Uncertain Futures

An Assessment of the Conditions of the Present

Uncertain Futures

An Assessment of the Conditions of the Present

Edmund Berger

Winchester, UK
Washington, USA

First published by Zero Books, 2017
Zero Books is an imprint of John Hunt Publishing Ltd., Laurel House, Station Approach,
Alresford, Hants, SO24 9JH, UK
office1@jhpbooks.net
www.johnhuntpublishing.com
www.zero-books.net

For distributor details and how to order please visit the 'Ordering' section on our website.

Text copyright: Edmund Berger 2016

ISBN: 978 1 78535 500 4
978 1 78535 501 1 (ebook)
Library of Congress Control Number: 2016941211

A CIP catalogue record for this book is available from the British Library.

Design: Stuart Davies

Printed and bound by CPI Group (UK) Ltd, Croydon, CR0 4YY, UK

We operate a distinctive and ethical publishing philosophy in all
areas of our business, from our global network of authors to
production and worldwide distribution.

CONTENTS

Introduction

In 2007, crisis struck the United States. The housing market, despite the insistences made by innumerable financial advisors and economists that it would continue to rise in value, bottomed-out. Following rapidly behind that were two additional houses of cards: on one hand, an increasingly monopolistic and interdependent system of financial capitalism, and on the other hand a wall of personal and corporate debt that had been mounting from the 1980s onward. If the mid-1990s were the boom-time of the "New Economy" – as described by its most excited advocates – then the mid-2000s marked its polar opposite. The national economy ground to a halt, while other economies bound up in this singular system began to crumble. As purchasing power collapsed in the United States, goods produced in export-oriented countries like China pooled up, gathering dust in factories, warehouses, and in the hulls of motionless transport ships. Commercial banks in Iceland defaulted and threw the country into a severe depression, while the financial contagion spread across Europe. It was there that the dominoes continued to fall: systemic problems in the economies of countries like Greece were peeled back, with emergency stabilization measures putting up roadblocks against effective alleviation means. Not all of this was the cause of the housing market of the United States – it was something far more systemic and intrinsic to the nature of globalized, integrated capitalism.

In the years following the crisis, many things have happened. Dictatorial regimes in the Middle East fell and people swarmed city centers and squares across the world in a resolute rejection of the system that had nearly robbed them of their livelihoods. Left-wing governments came to power in the countries that were hit the hardest, tried to strike out in a different direction, and had their goals rigorously dismantled by international organizations.

Bottom-up social and economic structures swelled in the cracks glossed over by the so-called recovery, and social-democratic leaders soared through the polls in countries where such an event was all but unimaginable.

These developments were met by near-opposite occurrences. Xenophobia and nationalism ripped through Europe, as the anger and fear created by the crisis was poured out on those deemed different. Far-right parties climbed up through the state apparatuses, and the sanctity of the border was declared against the flows of globalization. In the United States, right-wing populist sentiment organized first in support of libertarian policies intended to intensify the policies that aided in generating the crisis – and when that failed they turned towards economic and social nationalism. They now demand – like their European counterparts – the end of the era of globalization. From the left to the right, it appears that the "Washington Consensus" on political, social, and economic structures is on its way out. Paradoxically, it still stands strong and is poised to reclaim itself against those who contest it, no matter the nature of their dissent.

Situated in the immediate environment created by all of these events, it's easy to perceive them as random or freak occurrences. The crisis that officially began in 2007, from this perspective, appears as something unavoidable – had the proper policies been put into place. The rise of a left-wing consciousness, and the right-wing counterrevolution, appear as aberrations, temporary deviations from "business-as-usual" politics. The debate becomes, by extension, not one of the nature of this business in and of itself, but how best to define the "usualness" of this business. What would happen, however, if one was to suggest that the crisis emerged from within the system, by the very nature of its operations, and that the dueling perspectives engendered by its breaking point are precisely what is to be expected, in one form or another? One would then, quite naturally, have to raise questions as to the character of the "business" in the first place.

The perspective that crisis can be contextualized within the orderly operations of the system is precisely the analysis of capitalism offered by Karl Marx (it is unsurprising, then, that sales of Marx's books skyrocketed during the crisis!). Now largely neglected by a neoclassical economic orthodoxy that abstracts its models away from historical process, Marx, building on the classical economists before him, was amongst the first to take seriously the idea of the economy as a complex system. Furthermore, unlike the majority of the neoclassicals, this economic system was determined to be coupled to the social, political, and even ecological systems that it was embedded in, acting upon them as much as being acted upon. Most importantly for our purposes here, Marxist theory both directly and indirectly lays out a toolbox for approaching the questions of our time.

The goal of this work is threefold, with one aspect being expressed in each of the three chapters. The first chapter is to elucidate some key parts of Marx's theory (as well as relevant non-Marxist perspectives) in an easy and readable manner, and illustrate how it applies to contemporary economic history from the Great Depression to the Great Recession. The second chapter is to turn to the so-called "Washington Consensus" itself, to look at how it unfolded from its humble beginnings in 1930s Europe to its application in the United States between the 1980s and today. Just as the first chapter will stress how the future of capitalism as we currently know it is extremely fragile, the second argues quite similarly that the Washington Consensus, itself welded to capitalism's evolution, is splintering apart. Finally, the third chapter will consider the relationship between the current socio-economic situation and various important concepts: fascism, social democracy, socialism, reform, and revolution.

It must be stressed that the current work is not a comprehensive introduction to Marxist theory, nor an exhaustive history of American politics and economics. I have chosen a handful of concepts that I feel are relevant to describing our immediate present. From Marx these include surplus value, the organic composition of capital, and the rate of profit and its tendency to fall. From other economists I have brought in long-wave theory, which has its roots in Marxist economics but is applied quite often outside its methodology. If I neglected a concept or did not elucidate a concept to the full extent of its theoretical dimensions, it is not because I feel that the concept is irrelevant, but merely beyond the scope of what I've intended to be a rather short book. There are many brilliant writers, scholars, and activists who are doing paradigm-shifting research in the field of Marxist theory, and I would refer the interested reader to their efforts (alongside Marx's own texts) to gain a deeper understanding of the issues at hand. I have included these resources in the footnotes of each chapter.

Some might object that I've spent too much time focusing on the developments in the United States – particularly in the second chapter, essentially being an institutionalist history of American politics. This is simply because it is the country I've grown up in and is the country I know best. Much of that chapter stems from my own efforts to understand and come to terms with the trajectory of the country's political system, particularly the rise of forces such as the Tea Party, and more recently, Donald Trump. I try to touch on the events in other countries when necessary. Hopefully future studies will look at similar trajectories in other countries.

Chapter 1

From Then to Now

The Falling Rate of Profit

Marx's analysis of capitalism – and its tendency towards crisis – hinges on an analysis of what capitalism truly is. Indeed, innumerable tomes have been written by bourgeois economists to answer this very question. Certain schools of thought focus on the centrality of exchange, and the subsequent circulation of goods, in the construct that is referred to as "the market." Others look at capitalism from a moral perspective, arguing that it is the sign of free individuals interacting with one another in order to increase their own self-interests. Others still, taking cues from these, see it as a motor for development, the like of which has never been seen before in human history. Behind each of these approaches is one fundamental aspect, upon which Marx builds his own economic theory: capitalism, in its most recognizable form, is the private ownership over the means of production – that is, the ownership of the tools (in the broadest sense possible) to create the goods (or commodities) that circulate on the market. If one owns a given means of production, they are by default a capitalist. If you are employed by a capitalist, you are simply a worker. If we aggregate the owners of the means of production to encompass the economy of a whole, we reach the capitalist class – the bourgeoisie. Likewise, if we aggregate the workers employed by the bourgeoisie in a similar way, we reach the underclass – the proletariat.

What does the bourgeoisie do? As owners of the means of production, their role is to produce. This role, however, is not production for the sake of production. The goal of the individual capitalist is to sell the output of production on the market in exchange for money, the ultimate goal of which is to realize a profit. A portion of this profit goes back into production in order to allow production to continue. Another portion goes to the capitalist his or herself, increasing their own personal wealth. Because each capitalist looks to increase his or her personal wealth, the members of the bourgeoisie find themselves in a profound struggle with one another. Profit, then, must be realized and increased against the ebbs and flows of competition.

Due to competition, this rate of profit must always rise if the capitalist economy is to sustain itself. For the bourgeois economists, this is precisely what capitalism has done: continually increasing the rate of profit, constantly growing the economy (despite the occasional "misstep" or accident that results in recession or depression), and by extension, raising the standard of living for all. Even the poor, our economist says, are better off under capitalism than they would be in its void. Indeed, it was Marx and Engels who wrote in *The Communist Manifesto* that the "bourgeoisie, historically, has played a most revolutionary part" in development, "constantly revolutionizing the instruments of production" by creating "more massive and more colossal productions than have all preceding generations together."[1]

Yet can this rising rate of profit sustain itself? For early classical economists like Adam Smith and David Ricardo, the answer is no, even if they offered different and somewhat contradictory reasons. Marx, likewise, held that in the longest term possible, capitalism would exhibit a *falling rate of profit*. Marx finds in capitalism something akin to a thermodynamic system, always increasing in energy, but still tapered by the forces of entropy that lock it into a decline that will ultimately bring about its collapse.[2] This is not to say, of course, that capitalism's profit rates will exhibit a downward momentum if plotted on a historical graph. Capitalism, in order to realize profits, must always expand: new markets open up, new innovations enter into the markets, new consumers enter into the system, so on and so forth. Each of these, Marxian economists argue, can offset profit's fall, and set off again a rising rate of profit. Thus the proposed falling rate of profit would be a *tendency of the rate of profit to fall* (TRPF).

Does the TRPF exist? The massive wealth accumulation of the last hundred years would state otherwise, though as we will shortly see, some Marxian and non-Marxian economists suggest that there is a secular downward trend. The question then isn't simply whether or not the TRFP exists – but if it exists, does it help explain the events of the Great Recession, and by extension help us understand what comes next? In order to answer both of these questions, we have to look at why Marx believed the TRFP would take place. Before doing this, we must first review a thumbnail sketch of the basic tenets of Marxist economic theory, starting first with labor under capitalist conditions and its expression as *surplus value.*

The Birth of the Proletariat

In contemporary neoclassical economics, as in their predecessors, the marginalists, the issue of the relationship between labor and production is treated simply. Reaching its highest expression in the neo-marginalists associated with the Austrian School (the birthplace, as we see next chapter, of what constitutes political and economic "neoliberalism"), the worker agrees to labor for the capitalist in exchange for a monetary reimbursement – the wage. The nature of this binding agreement is, in the eyes of the neoclassical economists, a reflection of how they treat the capitalist system as a whole: a network of exchanges based on the buying and selling behaviors of free, rational agents. Like the buyer who purchases a commodity from the capitalist out of need or want, the worker similarly enters into a productive relationship with the capitalist in order to fulfil his or her own needs or wants.

This is not, Marx asserts, necessarily the case. The marginalists, the neo-marginalists and the neoclassicists as a whole treat capitalism as a sort of abstract principle: it appears as something detached from the world, a sort of idealized state of affairs. Marx's interpretation, by contrast, stresses capitalism as a mode of civilizational development that must be contextualized in its historical conditions. This means that the relationships between labor and production and the workers and the capitalist must too be historically situated, with particular attention paid to the development of the proletariat as a class. For Marx, it is only through the proletariat's development that one can properly understand what it is that the proletariat does.

Capitalism emerged from and supplanted feudalism, the dominant political and economic system in Europe between the 9th and 15th centuries. Under feudal relations, a large peasant class developed that served as the bottom-rung of the class ladder. Attaining a standard of living was contingent on the feudal lords, who would legally grant the peasants large tracts of land on which they could live and work. With this land, which might be collectively shared by entire peasant societies, the peasants owned their own means of production, which they utilized to create and sell goods. In exchange for the granting of this land, the lords and the Church would levy a heavy tax against the peasant classes – despite that, in perhaps the majority of cases, the land was in fact the peasants' ancestral land, having been seized by the lords through military conquest. Peasant revolts arose periodically through the Middle Ages, made possible by the vast amounts of land the class maintained. By the 1400s, both the Church and the wealthy classes began processes of expropriation and enclosure – the seizure of peasant land and its redistribution to the nobles, and the barring of the peasants from access to the commons. This process of dispossession would be repeated again with the advent of industrialization in the 18th century, this time with the aid of the state and the growing industrial classes. In this new dispossession, land became translated into *private property*, a commodity which could be then sold on the free market.[3]

By taking the land from the peasants, the peasants were effectively pauperized, shut off from their means of subsistence. Thus the former peasantry became transformed into the proletariat: robbed of their means of production and agricultural basis (and by extension, their ability to live), they would have to turn to the new industrial bourgeoisie, who had effectively subsumed and surpassed the former feudal nobility. By extension, the historical transformation of land into property via a process of commodification directly entailed the transformation of labor (as the ability to produce) into a commodity capable of being sold and bought in its own right. Far from being the freedom of exchange by free individuals (as neoclassicism poses), capitalism, by nature of its origins, maintained within itself the very relations of feudalism, effectively obscuring them in the dynamics of the market.

Surplus Value

What does the individual worker sell to the capitalist? Looking specifically at how the wage functions, Marx notes that it is not his or her labor that is being sold, but *labor-power*. Labor-power is different from labor in that it is not the act itself that is being sold, but *the capacity or possibility to do labor and to produce*. Once purchased by the capitalist, this labor-power is then directed into a relationship with the means of production (raw materials, factory equipment, tools, etc.) in order to produce production. The capitalist, effectively owning this product, can then sell it on the market. Part of the money exchanged (profit) goes back to the worker (wage); part goes into the means of production, and part goes to the capitalist. This obscures, however, another vital element in the process. The means of production impart a value, but significant value is added when the human laborer enters into the relation with the means of production. For example, wood, nails, lacquer, and metals have a value of their own, but it takes the force of labor-power to transform these elements into a table, which will then take on a value that is greater than the sum of its parts. It is the efforts of the laborer – and taken at aggregate, the proletariat as whole – that produce the value of the commodity form.

Critics of this labor theory of value have sometimes made the mistake of thinking that what Marx was arguing was the direct way in which the market value of a commodity is formed. This, however is an incorrect interpretation. In order to realize profit, the capitalist must sell the commodity at a higher price than the amount of value produced in the laboring process. If the commodity is sold, the capitalist accomplishes what Marxist theory maintains is a *realization of surplus value*. Realizing surplus value – which can only occur if and when the products of production are actively exchanged on the market for money – means that the capitalist has received more from production (that is, the creation and preserving of value by the worker) than he or she had initially put into production. In the case of the worker, on the other hand, all that has been received has been a wage which is ultimately lower than the value he or she imparted in the production process.

The labor theory of value can be unstated in other ways that allow it to be unpacked further. As American anarchist Benjamin Tucker wrote, "the natural wage of labor is its product."[4] This is the ultimate conclusion of the theory, and one can reason from his wording that what constitutes the modern wage would be, in fact, an unnatural wage. But why? The answer lies in the relationship between the value of labor-power, the wage, and the final outcome of labor-power put into action.[5] Let us say that the value of the labor-power is the wage, for it is labor-power that is being sold to the capitalist in order to meet the minimal necessary requirement for survival (that is, the commodities that lend one a quality of life). In modern society, the wage is largely correlated to time spent laboring, that is, the laborer receives a wage that represents the activities done within a single span of time worked. Let's assume, in a given scenario, that the daily wage of the laborer is represented by the number 6, representing directly the value of the labor-power. To use our earlier example of the table, let's assume that it takes 8 hours of *living labor* to produce a table, with an additional 6 hours of *embodied labor* (labor that has been done in the past) to produce the raw materials necessary for the construction of the table.

In this scenario, the manufacturing of the table has combined the 8 hours of living labor with the 6 hours of past labor, giving us a final value of 14. The formula for this, if we are inclined towards using one, is $EL + LL = W$, the EL representing embodied labor, the LL representing living labor, and W being the final value – in this case, 14. The living labor, however, can be broken down into two parts. If we recall that the labor-power was 6, we can see that in the construction of the table (using 8 hours of living labor) this value was imparted with an addition value of 2 – the surplus value. This means that the laborer has carried out both paid labor and unpaid labor over the course of the table's construction. The formula, then, should be $EL + LLp + LLu = W$, with LLp and LLu being paid living labor and unpaid living labor, respectively. It follows, as the forces of competition wear at the capitalist, that he or she is compelled to eliminate portions from the labor pool and speed up the amount of production done with a given amount of labor-power. Thus, in the long run the capitalist firm subjects the worker to an increasing *rate of exploitation*, itself bound to the firm's *rate of profit*.

The ultimate purpose, as stated above, is that under the capitalist system the paid living labor can never close the gap with unpaid living labor, for the vanishing of surplus value would entail the elimination of the role of private ownership over the means of production – and with its passing, the entire edifice of class society would vanish too. Furthermore, the gap between paid and unpaid labor reveals another fundamental aspect of capitalist society, one rarely if ever mentioned: that the act of material labor is the true source of wealth, being that which produces the value of manufacturing's output. All other forms of wealth income – from the kind received in the form of profits, to the kind received in the form of rent, to the kind received in the form of stocks, interests, dividends, what have you – constitute a distribution arising from the *accumulation of surplus value* after it has been received in the form of money at the point of sale. These relations are ultimately mystified by the tendency towards universalization by bourgeois morality, traditions, and norms, divorcing this system's relationship to historical processes and making it an affair of voluntary contracts. To quote Andrew Kliman, "From within the standpoint of present-day society, there is nothing to criticize. The exploitation of the worker can only be criticized from the standpoint of the possible non-exploitative, classless society of the future."[6]

The Organic Composition of Capital and the Rate of Profit

We can now turn our attention to two other elements in Marxist theory: the organic composition of capital (OCC) and the rate of profit (ROP). The relationship between the OCC and the ROP, and between each of these with the rate of surplus value, are among the central aspects of Marxist political economy, as they stand as his framework for determining and measuring the dynamics of the capitalist system when taken as a whole. Furthermore, each element is required to approach Marx's theory of the TRPF.

When considering the production process in singular, we find two different forms of capital at work. The first of these is what Marx calls *constant capital*, by which he means the capital outlays associated with fixed assets (machines and tools), the raw materials needed for production, incidental expenses, etc. This corresponds in many respects to what neoclassical economists call the "factors of production," which is the total number of inputs that go into the production process. Marxist economic theory differs in that it breaks these inputs down into different types of capital. Besides constant capital, Marx identifies what he calls "variable capital," which is the costs associated with buying labor-power from the worker. The total cost of constant and variable capital would be total costs associated with production, which must then be measured against the realization of surplus value in order to determine the ROP. Marx represents the ROP with the following formula: $P = S / C + V$ wherein P represents the ROP, S represents the amount of surplus value realized, C represents constant capital, and V represent variable capital.

Embedded in this formula is OCC, the organic composition of capital. This is simply the ratio of constant capital to variable capital – C / V. This formula is used to measure the difference between the rate of surplus value and the rate of profit. We can note that there is a tension that exists between the OCC and the ROP, as the OCC represents investments forwarded by the capitalist in anticipation of returns higher than these outlays. This becomes problematic when one takes into account the role of competition between capitalists, each vying for larger and larger rates of surplus value. For an individual capitalist to maintain a rising ROP, larger and larger investments must be poured into constant and variable capital – or more commonly, cutting variable capital while increasing constant capital. The capitalist, in other words, invests in more and better machines that speed up the production process, make better commodities, and/or carry out the work with fewer workers.

Developments such as these usually begin in a single capitalist firm, and when successful give the capitalist a competitive advantage relative to his or her competitors. Taken at a specific moment (most commonly at the beginning of a business cycle), the rising OCC triggers a rising ROP. As the new tools and techniques matriculate through the sector of the economy and become standard means of production, this picture starts to change: competition gains on the innovative capitalist, whose

ROP begins to decline. Therefore, the higher the OCC in a given industry (which today would be defined as a *capital-intensive* industry), the lower the ultimate rate of profit.

For these reasons, Marx maintained that capitalism, when taken as a stage of historical development, would suffer the falling rate of profit. Now, it must be noted that Marx did not think that the TRPF would be an ongoing and gradual force (as Adam Smith held), nor did he necessarily think it would be noticeable without careful attention paid to the passage of historical time. As stated earlier, counter-tendencies will be introduced into capitalism to cause rapid expansion in the rate of surplus value, setting off large rates of profit. Writing in the 1960s, for example, Marxist economists Paul Baran and Paul Sweezy introduced what they called simply the "surplus," referencing the massive wealth accumulation through mechanisms such as luxury goods, yearly automobile industries, the advertising industries, and planned obsolescence.[7] Writing in his own time, Marx observed that these counter-tendencies most frequently present themselves in the wake of economic crises and other cataclysmic events (such as wars), as investment begins to flow and replace capital that may have been destroyed. It is interesting to note, then, that Baran and Sweezy's "surplus" emerged in the wake of a long and violent set of crises – the Great Depression and the Second World War. Yet Baran and Sweezy did not think that the surplus was without a set of contradictions that would undermine it: if accumulated, the surplus (centralizing more and more in large, monopolistic firms) would eventually over-extend itself and outpace the number of spaces where it could be "absorbed." As they write:

> [Monopoly capitalism] tends to generate ever more surplus, yet it
> fails to provide the consumption and investment outlets required for
> the absorption of a rising surplus and hence for the smooth working
> of the system. Since surplus which cannot be absorbed will not be

produced, it follows that the normal state of the monopoly capitalist economy is stagnation.[8]

This is, of course, a fundamentally different reason for the TRFP, emphasizing not the rising OCC against the ROP, but the limitations of realizing a rising OCC against a veritable "wall of wealth." At the same time, one might pose that this particular tendency anticipated by Baran and Sweezy was unique to their historical conditions, that is, the capitalism of the postwar boom. Either way, hypothesizing a TRPF is something completely different from providing evidence that such a phenomenon, in a generalized and capitalism-wide way, is occurring. Empirical evidence should exist that confirms or refutes the theory.

The research of Marxist economist Michael Roberts has provided steps towards this. Taking data provided by the US government, he deploys Marx's formula of $P = S / C + V$ by using the following information inputs: S is the US net national product minus employee compensation, C is net fixed assets (excluding the public sector), and V is employee compensation including benefits.[9] His extrapolation from Marx found the expected cycles of rising and falling ROP since the Great Depression. From 1945 to 1965, the era of the postwar boom, the ROP was rising, followed by a falling ROP running from 1965 to 1982. Another rising ROP took off again in 1982, before falling again in 1997 – a trend that would follow right through the Great Recession. Importantly, Robert's evidence illustrates that periods of rising ROP reflected a falling OCC and vice versa. Even more importantly, it would appear that each successive period of rising ROP *is lower than the period of rising ROP that preceded it*, with recovery time from each period of falling ROP becoming more protracted. There is, in other words, evidence that there is a tendency for the rate of profit to fall.

Robert's findings have been confirmed by other economists using a variety of tools.[10] Simon Mohun, for example, finds rising

ROP running from 1946 to 1965, a decline through 1982, and another peak in 1997 – a tendency more or less equal to the one that Roberts found. George Economakis, Alexis Anastasiadis, and Maria Markak, likewise, found a similar pattern of rising ROP from 1946 to 1966, a fall from 1966 to 1983, with a peak and subsequent fall occurring in 1997. Andrew Kliman, utilizing a separate set of metrics based on corporate profits, has also produced his own model that shows an overall decline across the modern era.[11] A very similar succession of turns, with a margin of differentiation, can be found when we turn our attention to the patterns of bull markets (upward trends in financial markets) and bear markets (downward trends in financial markets). Shimshon Bichler and Jonathan Nitzan[12] have found that a bear market ran from 1928 to 1948, with a bull market kicking off and running until 1968. At this point the financial markets turned, with a bear market continuing until a turn-around in 1981. The following bull continued on through 1999, before settling into bear that lasted up through the Great Recession.

The capitalist system is an international phenomenon, particularly in regards to our current moment that is so eloquently framed by commentators as the "era of globalization." It would stand, then, that the TRPF should be able to be viewed from not simply the vantage point of the United States, but the world economy as a whole. Indeed, several Marxist economists affiliated with the *Journal for World Systems Research* utilized data from the US, Great Britain, Japan and the EU (when available) to chart out a world rate of profit.[13] The findings corresponded roughly with the tendency found in the US: a rising rate of profit from 1940 to 1969, a falling rate from 1970 to 1983, and another rising rate that peaked in 1998. Furthermore, each peak of the rising ROP was found to be lower than the previous peak. Roberts has produced similar results by data from each of the G7 nations (Canada, France, Germany, Great Britain, Italy, and Japan, plus the United States) and the BRIC nations (Brazil,

Russia, India, and China). This revealed that the world hit a peak in profitability that bottomed out in 1975, with a peak again in the mid-90s. Importantly, the world has yet to be able to achieve the sorts of profits realized in 1963. At the same time, Roberts notes a divergence between the rates of profit of the developing world (represented by the BRIC nations) and the developed world (represented by the G7), with the developing countries playing a fundamental role in the driving of the world ROP.

Underconsumption and Overproduction

The General Formula of Capital

When Marx speaks of the "general formula of capital,"[14] he defines it quite simply. On one hand is the commodity circle, represented as C-M-C, with C representing the commodity and M representing money. The commodity, in other words, yields money (through profits realized at the point of sale), which becomes new commodities by feeding back into production. Alongside C-M-C exists another cycle: M-C-M'. This follows the transformation of money into the commodity, which then begets money that exceeds the initial amount of money – hence M'. For capitalism to continually function, as we saw in the previous section, the capitalist must constantly produce M' through the extraction of surplus value.

One way in which the capitalist attempts to realize M', as we've just seen, is through rising the organic composition of capital – sometimes with detrimental effects, setting off the tendency for the rate of profit to fall. At play in a rising OCC can be a tendency to pour more investments into constant capital than variable capital; that is, replacing human labor-power with labor-saving machines. Given that the selling of labor-power is necessary for consumption (and thus for M to become M'), this is a critical contradiction in the dynamics of the capitalist system, particularly in our era of smart machines and increasing automation. This contradiction between constant and variable capital is indicative of the fundamental tension between the workers and the owners of the means of production.

This tension should alert us to another aspect of the unequal relationship between the worker and capitalist. As we saw earlier, the worker's labor-power is traded for a wage, and is then put to work producing commodities that exchange on the market in excess of the worker's wage. The formula of M-C-M' therefore requires that the worker's wages or compensation must be kept at a minimum (this is the reason why the capitalist class has historically rejected unionization and minimum-wage increases). To put it simply, the worker must sell their labor-power at *wholesale price*, with the products of their labor-power put to work then being sold on the market at *retail price*. The question becomes one, then, as to whether or not the working class taken in aggregate, constituting the majority of the population (and thus the consuming base by extension), can purchase what they produce at a rate capable of sustaining M-C-M' in the long run. This question becomes more essential as the OCC rises through the introduction of mass-manufacturing techniques, which can pump out greater and greater amounts of commodities on the market while lowering the value added. If the rate of purchasing power cannot cope with this scenario, hypothetically speaking, then capitalism will suffer a *crisis of underconsumption*.

Underconsumption and its Discontents

While Marxist economists have often endorsed underconsumption theories, it should be pointed out that Marx himself did not believe that underconsumption was a valid explanation for the development of crises. This is because underconsumption, from Marx's perspective, is not an occasional event, but a constant aspect of capitalism as a whole. As Engels writes:

the under-consumption of the masses, the restriction of the

consumption of the masses to what is necessary for their mainte-
nance and reproduction, is not a new phenomenon. It has existed as
long as there have been exploiting and exploited classes... The
under-consumption of the masses is a necessary condition of all
forms of society based on exploitation, consequently also of the
capitalist form.[15]

At the same time, however, Engels does not write off underconsumption in full, noting that it is a prerequisite condition of
crises, and plays in them a role which has long been recognized.

If underconsumption theory has a father, it is Jean Charles
Leonard de Sismondi, a Swiss economist who lived from 1773 to
1842.[16] For Sismondi, the disconnection between the profits
accrued by the wealthy and the poverty of the working classes
was a contradiction that threatened the stability of the fledgling
capitalist system. Instability could be attributed to what he called
a "general glut"[17] – a situation where production would generate
a situation of *overproduction*, in which the working class could
never consume in a way to keep the rate of profit up. In such a
scenario, supply would outstrip demand – a recognition that led
Sismondi to see it as a problem for both supply-side economics
and demand-side economics. While he was not a socialist in any
way, Sismondi's theories became the foundation of many non-
Marxist socialist critiques of capitalism, and influenced Marx
himself greatly.

Sismondi's general theory of underconsumption stood in stark
contrast to the leading economic theories of his time, which
rallied behind what was called "Say's Law," developed by the
French economist Jean-Baptiste Say. In Say's Law it follows that
the underconsumption glut is impossible because supply always
and absolutely generates its own demand – a conclusion the
economist reached by asserting that overproduction could only
occur in relation to the dynamics of supply. Simply put, there
could be a situation in which, say, the number of table tops could

be double that of available table legs. This disproportionality could only exist temporarily, Say suggests, because this would entail a doubling in the manufacturing of table legs to meet the demands of production: "the mere circumstance of creation of one product immediately opens a vent for other products."[18]

This, of course, does not properly address Sismondi's critique in that the law remains largely focused on the supply-side. It does not address a situation in which a shortage of money, arising either through the low wages paid to the workers or through the workers' elimination from the productive process (or a combination of the two), makes it impossible to fully consume the supply. It would be David Ricardo, a supporter of Say's Law, who would tackle this problem. Again, it is the tendency towards balance that forms the basis of the solution, which comes in here at the point of sale. If the abundance of goods cannot be purchased at their current prices, Ricardo posits, then there would be a fall in the rate of nominal prices in order to assure that the orderly pattern of production and consumption could continue onward unabated. Thus, just as differences in supply would reach a balance, so too would both supply and demand find themselves in balance.

Say's Law and Ricardo's additions point towards what is called the "general equilibrium theory," innovated at different points by the marginalists and neoclassical economists such as Leon Walras and Vilfredo Pareto, which maintains the possibility of a balance between many different markets, between the different sectors of production, and by extension, between the productive sector and the labor market. While significant differences between the Ricardians and the marginalists exist, we can see that they remain unified in a trajectory of economic thought that holds that the capitalist market, taken as a whole (defined by Walras as a state of perfect competition, which for him was an impossibility), is a self-organizing system that will tend towards the betterment of all who participate in it.

It must be asked if this is actually the case of the capitalist system. One vigorous critique of these suppositions, targeting Say's Law explicitly, was the economic theory of John Maynard Keynes. Keynes, in fact, flips Say on his head: it is not supply that determines demand, but consumption that determines the conditions of the production of this supply. At the same time, Keynes was doubtful that production of supply would be capable of maintaining full employment, which would set off a downward spiral in which unemployment would pull down the possibility of the supply being consumed, leading to greater rates of unemployment. This leads Keynes to break with the theories of self-organizing balance, and endorse a variation of the underconsumption theories of Sismondi (though his point of reference is the reactionary economist Thomas Robert Malthus, himself a follower of Sismondi). The Keynesian solution is to increase the possibilities of demand through welfare, job-growth programs, and other forms of government stimulus enabled through deficit spending. Only through successful government intervention, Keynes argued, could the capitalist economy reach something that looked like an equilibrium based on full employment.

Keynesian theory was forged in the context of economic crisis, most specifically the British unemployment crisis of the 1920s. Adversarial to socialism and Marxism in particular, Keynes worked closely with the British government in developing jobs programs – but it would be in the wake of the Great Depression that his theories would find their highest application, becoming the de facto economic paradigm of choice for both the US and European governments. It appeared to be wildly successful: for the US economy, the Keynesian era saw the highest peak in the rate of profit in the modern history of capitalism (1963), the lowest unemployment rate (1969), and the longest bout of income equality (between roughly 1960 and 1970). In this time period, Keynes came to if not replace Marx then parallel him in terms of relevancy in the eyes of many Marxist theorists and socialist organizations, most notably the *Monthly Review* school of Paul Baran and Paul Sweezy. This marked a redirection of aims for many socialists, a movement from the abolishment of capitalism to one of "smoothing out" capitalism's contradictions. If full employment and the standard of living could be increased within capitalism, alongside a repudiation of the tendency of the rate of profit to fall, then the need for revolutionary theory was all but abolished.

At the end of the 60s, however, something funny happened: Keynesianism ran headlong into a crisis, one that would open the floodgates for the neoliberal system that we are currently moored within. Inflation rose considerably, and would transform into a decade-long stagflation that threatened the longevity of the capitalist project itself. The rate of profit declined, having yet to truly recover. Government expenditures threw the dollar into crisis, and the inflexibility of production, particularly in the face of foreign competition, sent shockwaves through the global market. Importantly, this crisis saw no decline in demand and real evidence of a "general glut" of commodities. Does this mean that the underconsumption theories are incorrect, or that the Keynesian approach is not applicable (from the perspective of the capitalist)? Not precisely. To answer this, we must turn to one of the largest crises of modern capitalism: the Great Depression.

Uneven Development

In the second volume of *Capital*, Marx divides industrial capitalism into two "departments." The first of these, Department I, constitutes the production of the means of production: raw materials, machinery, and the like (in other words, constant capital). Department II, on the other hand, is the output of production proper: consumer goods, luxury items, and other commodities. It is between Department I and II that a critical imbalance can occur, raising the specter of more generalized crises of overproduction and underconsumption. Unlike

Say and Ricardo, Marx saw the possibility of overproduction occurring in Department I,[19] a situation that takes on larger dimensions when we factor in the inevitable rise in the organic composition of capital, which can be compounded by the general underconsumption that is necessary for capitalism – a potent combination that can trigger the arrival of a crisis. An argument can be made that this is precisely what occurred in the build-up to the Great Depression.

The early 1900s saw the introduction of a wide-scale transformation in the modes of production, made possible by developments in the technologies in production and the invention of "Taylorism," that is, the so-called "scientific management" of labor that aimed to increase worker productivity through processes of regimentation and standardization.[20] This new production mode introduced semi-automated systems, typified by the assembly line created by Henry Ford in his automobile factories in Detroit and the "flexible mass production" introduced by Alfred Sloan at General Motors. Under the Fordist paradigm, the mass production of similar commodities became the golden standard of industrial capitalism, calling into being simultaneously a new regime of social regulation (including the rise of the advertising industries, "industrial" psychology, higher stages of organizational planning in both the corporate firm and the state, and the reinforcement of values and ethics deemed equitable to maintaining the rates of production). In the immediate context of labor, Fordism greatly accelerated the rate of surplus value extraction, and by extension accelerated the production of commodities.

The rise of advertising, business psychology, planning, and the like signals a shift from pre-Fordist capitalism, where the output of limited production was focused primarily on scattered, localized markets, to one in which national markets were essential to maintain the solvency of American capitalism, entailing by extension the need for the laborer to be able to consume more and more of this output. Measures were taken to ensure that this occurred; Ford himself, famously, raised the daily pay in his factories to $5 (though it has to be pointed out that half of this increase came in the form of bonuses, which the workers were only entitled to after being approved by Ford's Socialization Organization – a firm that would routinely check on worker's private lives to ensure they were living the "American Way"). During the 1920s, wages climbed alongside the rapid expansion of credit to the working class (innovated primarily by General Motor's auto loans). It appeared successful: between 1920 and 1929, income obtained from profit (realization of surplus value), rents, and interest climbed 45%, while total wealth accumulated by the country's wealthiest soared to dizzying heights.[21] The apparent success of the "roaring 20s" became a "business euphoria."

This euphoria obscured the reality of the uneven development that had been amplified by the introduction of Fordism. The boom led to extreme income inequality: by 1929 the top 0.1% of the population held a combined income equal to the bottom 45%. For all the talk of wage increases, the decade leading up to the Great Depression saw the wage income of the working class increase by only 13%. This meant that despite the speeding-up of production through labor-saving technology, the development of national markets, and the easy availability of credit, it became harder and harder for capitalists to realize surplus value as profit. In 1926, three years prior to the Great Depression, the consumer commodity market witnessed a peak and a decline, indicating the building of an underconsumption crisis tearing at the relationship between supply and demand.

The uneven development between the conditions of production and the conditions of society exacerbated an uneven development between the departments of production. Anticipating a long-term rising rate of demand, investments – inflated by the proliferation of credit – poured into Department I.

Anticipating a rise in prices alongside this demand, a wave of commodity and money speculations spread across the market as a whole. As Michel Aglietta points out, this generated a situation where "[f]inancial circulation [began] to exhibit an autonomous movement of its own," wholly detached from the distortions between production and consumption on one side, and between the two departments on the other.[22] In the years between 1923 and 1926, the output of Department I doubled the rate of productive capacity in Department II. What this meant was that when consumption peaked and declined in 1926, a surplus had built up that could not be absorbed, triggering a decline in investments. This difficulty in realizing surplus value as profit triggered the flow of more and more capital into finance, leading the nominal value of financial firms to increase from $100 million in 1924 to $1800 million in 1929. This mountain of wealth, however, was built upon an increasingly shaky foundation: a literal wall of debt had formed, with speculation becoming the only way of realizing any sort of potential profit. This is the situation that exploded on October 22nd, 1929, ushering in the Great Depression.

The Long Wave

Juglar, Kitchin, Kondratiev
In his 1939 book *Business Cycles*,[23] Schumpeter sought to carry out a synthesis of the different business cycle theories that had been circulating through economic thought, honing in on three primary cycles that he felt contained the explanation for the oscillations between prosperity and depression. These were the *Juglar cycles* (identified in 1862 by Clement Juglar), the *Kitchin cycles* (discovered in the 1920s by Joseph Kitchin), and the *Kondratiev wave* (described by Nikolai Kondratiev in 1925). Each cycle, all exhibiting their own patterns of rise, peak, and decline, unfolds in different amounts of time: the Juglar cycle plays out across

seven to ten years, while the Kitchin cycle is considerably shorter, lasting roughly forty to forty-two months. The Kondratiev wave, on the other hand, spans fifty to sixty years, with the peak of the wave occurring around the middle.

Juglar, Kitchin, and Kondratiev waves all correspond to different movements in capitalist production. The Juglar cycle arises from capital investments in the production process, particularly where the actual conditions of the modes of production, alongside the raw materials for production, are concerned. This cycle had already been discovered, in fact, by Marx, in the *Grundrisse* (a point readily acknowledged by Schumpeter). For Marx, this was the ten-year *industrial cycle*, which he defines as "periods of moderate activity, prosperity, over-production, stagnation, and crisis."[24] Indeed, Schumpeter notes that the Juglar cycle is intricately bound to crisis, with a depression and recession occurring at the bottom of the cycle's downswing. Furthermore, given that this cycle deals with investments in production, there should exist a correlation between the cycle and the periods in which the organic composition of capital rises.

The Kitchin cycle, on the other hand, arises from the inventory stock held by capitalist firms. In times of prosperity, capitalist firms will increase the output of production, which will inevitably lead to a flood of commodities on the marketplace. In the Kitchin cycle, overproduction occurs as the amount of available commodities effectively outstrips demand and inventory stocks remain full – yet a time lag appears to develop between suppliers and manufacturers. This time lag, in turn, becomes coupled with a generalized slow-down of production until existing inventory stocks run down. Importantly, Schumpeter suggests, the Juglar cycle and Kitchin cycles usually alternate in their peaks and troughs. In other word, prosperity rising in the Juglar cycle can offset a crisis generated by a declining Kitchin cycle and vice versa.

The Kondratiev wave encompasses the Juglar and Kitchin

cycles, with a succession of these minor cycles occurring within the course of a single Kondratiev. It can best be described as a long-term wave of capitalist expansion, complete with its own rise, peak, stagnation, and recession. This overall wave, however, exhibited two phases, with a crisis – or "turning point" – marking the transition between one phase and the next. Writing in the 1920s, Kondratiev identified three waves spanning the development of modern capitalism: the first running from 1790 to 1849, with a turning point in 1815; the second running from 1850 to 1896, with a turning point in 1873; and a third one (for Kondratiev, the then-current wave) kicking off in 1896. The problem arises, however, when one asks what exactly sets off this long wave. For Kondratiev, the explanation was to be found in patterns of capital investment, while Schumpeter argued that the wave was the very force of *creative destruction* that he saw as the dynamic underlying capitalism itself. At the start of each wave, he posited, one would find a paradigm-shifting innovation that forcibly changed every sector of the market (we should point out that this implies, by default, an extremely important role for investment). Neo-Schumpeterian perspectives, such as those offered by Christopher Freeman and Carlota Perez,[25] have gone to considerable lengths in identifying the role that innovation plays in the long wave, suggesting that each wave is the expansion – and eventual exhaustion – of a given technological revolution. For Freeman and Perez, the turning point signifies the movement from the "installation period," in which industry undergoes rapid transformations, to a "deployment period," in which the contradictions and uneven developments of the installation period are smoothed out.

Different economists have posed different dates in their periodization, but for the time being let us use Perez and Freeman's own dates. In their schema, we can discern at least three eras immediately relevant to our concerns here. These are the "Age of Steel and Heavy Engineering," running from around

1875 to 1907; the "Age of Mass Production," running from 1908 to 1970; and the "Age of Information-Communication Technology," itself kicking off in 1970 and going on through today. Each tends towards the triad of phases: in the Age of Steel and Heaving Engineering, we can discern an installation phase between 1875 and 1889, a turning point between 1890 and 1894, and a deployment running from 1895 to the installation phase of the Age of Mass Production in 1908. The following turning point occurred from 1929 to 1943, and the resulting deployment phase concluded in 1970. In our present Age of Information-Communication Technology, we witnessed a long installation phase running from 1970 up through 2007, with the crisis marking the inauguration of the turning point – which we are arguably still within. It must be noted, importantly, that each turning point coincides with systemic economic crisis: in the Age of Steel and Heavy Engineering, this was the crisis of the 1890s; for the Age of Mass Production, it was the Great Depression. Finally, in the Age of Information-Communication Technology, it has been, of course, the Great Recession.

It is beyond our scope here to address the question of periodization, though it is certainly a question to be taken up at a future point. What should be of interest to us is the problem that long-wave theories pose to economics, both neoclassical and Marxist alike. For the neoclassical economist, the idea that capitalist development can be plotted into interlacing waves, each exhibiting their own rises, peaks, and falls, runs contrary to the notion that capitalism tends towards equilibrium. For the Marxist, on the other hand, the reoccurrence of capitalist expansion appears as a profound contradiction of the tendency of the rate of profit to fall. This proposition assumes, of course, that the "golden age" (i.e. the deployment period) of each wave produces a rate of profit on par with or larger than the previous expansionary wave. It is only interesting to recall early Michael Robert's determination, using Marx's formula, that there was a rising rate of profit, with a corollary low organic composition of capital, between 1945 and 1965 (corresponding to a bull market, indicating that the finance markets were responding favorably). This is precisely the time period identified by Perez as the "golden age" in the era of mass production. The resolution of this era, and the turn towards the next long wave, corresponds with a bear market, a rising organic composition of capital, and a falling rate of profit.

Further questions arise when we consider the specific causes of the new waves. It is readily apparent that the introductions of paradigm-shifting innovations (such as the steam engine, the automobile, the computer, etc.) are the pivots of these tendencies; both Kondratiev and later Schumpeter observed that during the stagnating points of a wave innovations tended to "pool" together, finding only marginal application in the economy due to low investments. The innovations that would set off the Age of Mass Production first entered into circulation in the deployment phase of the Age of Steel and Heavy Engineering, just as the computer, so essential for the Age of Information-Communication Technology, became prominent first in the deployment stage of the Age of Mass Production. Remaining at the perspective of bourgeois producer, Schumpeter chooses to simply attribute an increasing rate of investment as the force that brings these innovations to their full realization. Yet as we established at the outset of this chapter, investment must follow a rising rate of profit, and thus follow the realization of surplus value. This itself indicates a transformation involving the relations of production – and indeed, Christopher Freeman sees turning points as the opportunity for "institutional adaptation" that must be successfully carried out if the deployment phase is to take root.[26] For Freeman, institutional adaptation entails the "updating" of the "socio-institutional framework" of a given historical era to cope with the new conditions arising from the technological revolution. This explanation, of course, remains again abstracted from labor, and does not acknowledge that any "socio-institutional frameworks" will be marked with the struggles inherent to class society – as will any "golden age" of successful deployment. So what drives the turning point, and allows for the renewed realization of surplus value? To unpack this, we must now turn to the postwar boom.

Evening Out

As we saw earlier, the Great Depression emerged in the context of a crisis of underconsumption, one that encompassed both the relationship between producers and consumers and the relationship between the two departments of production. It was thus generated by the contradictions inherent to both its unique historical moment – the introduction of mass production into a plane of uneven social development – and the greater capitalist system, that is, the chronic inevitability of general underconsumption and the tendency of the rate of profit to fall. Importantly, it is easily observable that while the "deployment phase" of the previous age (the Age of Steel and Heavy Engineering) saw a surging mass of profits for the wealthy, society itself remained underdeveloped and dogged by persistent depression. This "long depression," as it has been called, set off the great global race of colonialism, as nations hunted for cheaper raw materials to increase their profits – thus putting into motion the events that would erupt into World War I. This period also saw an explosion in workers' struggle, typified by the trade-union movement in the United States but also the Russian Revolution, which ultimately brought the Soviets to power.

This empowering of class conscious would play a fundamental role in the resolution of the Great Depression (the "institutional adaptation"). This would be President Roosevelt's New Deal, with its moves to push back against the power of finance capital, its courting of the labor movement, its utilization of welfare and jobs programs, and its ushering in of the Keynesian consensus. From this perspective, the New Deal constitutes a major victory for the working class, even if one of the primary goals was to re-channel class consciousness into a reformist platform. Despite these efforts, there was a steady incline of labor strikes across the 1960s, right in the heart of the Keynesian program. As the economist Michal Kalecki has shown, the business classes grew increasingly worried during the 1960s, as policies promoting full employment appeared to be empowering the working class to take more radical and adversarial stances.[27] When combined with the Civil Rights movement, the students' movements and the widespread opposition to the Vietnam War, a broad, if informal, coalition against the Fordist paradigm could be traced.

It must be asked, however, to what extent the New Deal truly played a role in ameliorating the conditions of the Great Depression. The first New Deal was applied in 1933, almost immediately following Roosevelt's election; its mix of fiscal conservatism (intended to reduce federal deficits by cutting government worker wages, as in the Economy Act of March 20th, 1933) and the managerial-style cartelization of industry (best exemplified by the National Recovery Administration, which reduced competition between firms and implemented price controls) appeared to have been successful. The economy began growing at an accelerating rate, but virulent opposition – led primarily by conservative businessmen – began to dismantle Roosevelt's sets of programs. He responded in 1935 with the second New Deal, which entailed the Social Security Act, the National Labor Relations Act, and the creation of the Work Progress Administration. Again, the economy appeared to grow, with production reaching its 1929 levels in early 1937.

Then it went awry: in mid-1937 the economy took a sharp downturn. Industrial production fell by 30%, and by 1938 unemployment rates had grown from 14.3% to 19.0%.[28] Roosevelt was quick to blame monopoly capital for obstruction recovery, and led the FBI to launch an investigation into business practices. It would seem, however, that this was not the case. In 1938, the rate of profit for US corporations was below half of that in 1929, while investments were just barely above their levels at the outbreak of the Great Depression. What this indicates is that surplus value was not being realized at a rate high enough to drive up the rate of profit, and thus set off a wave of investments that could grow the economy. This means that the New Deal was, in actuality, *incapable of resolving the contradictions of Fordist capitalism and thus unable to resolve the crisis of the Great Depression.* This challenges the neo-Schumpterian theories of "institutional adaptation" as something *endogenous* (that is, emerging from within) to the forces of the long wave.

If it was not the New Deal, then what brought about a resolution to the crisis? The rate of profit for corporations sharply climbed in 1941, coupled with a doubling of investments as a share of GDP. This was not due to the New Deal stimulus programs, but to the entry of the United States into the Second World War. Fueled by higher taxation rates and deficit spending, the government plowed huge sums of money into industrial production, retooling American automobile companies to produce tanks and the like and building up the armaments industry. The war effort overseas and the needs of production at home cut down unemployment; wages were increased but domestic consumption was discouraged and channeled instead into war bonds and saving. The moribund capitalist-market economy became, in other words, a capitalist-war economy capable of delivering the "shock" necessary to resolving critical contradictions eating at the system. That war continually destroyed the output of production (i.e. the machinery produced for war), the needs for industrial production only amplified over the course of the conflict.

When the war ended, the US economy experienced a set of recessions, first in 1945 and again in 1948–1949, the latter of which was expected by many to be a resumption of the Great Depression. Instead, the economy rebounded and set off the long postwar boom, save for several minor slumps attributable to the ending of industrial cycles (i.e. the Juglar waves). Again this was attributed to the ascendency of Keynesianism as the dominant economic paradigm of the US and much of the Western World – yet as with the case of the New Deal, the reality is in fact not so straight-forward. While it is true that Keynesian-inspired policies assisted in mitigating the effects of the minor slumps and assisted in raising the standard of living, there are multiple historical factors that must be taken into consideration. The first of these was the build-up of savings during the war: with rationing removed, capital flowed back into consumer goods, greatly assisting the reconversion of industry from war demand to consumer demand. More important perhaps was the role played by the destruction wrought by the war, which saw production decimated in Western Europe and Asia. As the reconstructions began, these spaces became open markets for US goods. Production levels steadily increased to cope with the demands of these exports, accelerating the rate of surplus value and the rate of profit. For both domestic markets and international markets, the research and development carried out during wartime had generated numerous new innovations that assisted in realizing higher rates of investment and return. Finally, the Cold War played an essential role in this boom by ushering in an unprecedented arms build-up, which funneled billions into the defense industries. The social democracy of the Keynesian era was, in other words, simply a new form of the war economy.

Does this mean that the long-wave theory is ultimately incorrect? Not exactly. What this indicates is that the "turning point," when manifesting as a contradiction-wrought crisis, may very well need exogenous (i.e. outside) factors in order to properly spark a recovery. In the case of the "long boom," it appears that what occurred was in fact abnormal to the capitalist system. Had such a wide of swath of destruction not been cut across the face of the earth, it is unlikely that recovery could have achieved the rates of profit that it did. This problem of exogenous factors was, in fact, part and parcel of Trotsky's own critique of Kondratiev's initial theory of the long wave. As he wrote:

The acquisition by capitalism of new countries and continents, the discovery of new natural resources, and, in the wake of these, such major facts of 'superstructural' order as wars and revolutions determine the character and the replacement of ascending, stagnating or declining epochs of capitalist development. Along what path then should investigation proceed? To establish the curve of capitalist development in its non-periodic (basic) and periodic (secondary) phases and to breaking points in respect to individual countries of interest to us and in respect to the entire world market.[29]

To recap: the Fordist mass-production techniques were introduced (or, in the neo-Schumpterian parlance, "installed") into a highly underdeveloped social and economic system, exacerbating the contradictions that were present. This strain set off a wave of speculation that quickly detached itself from the material conditions of production, resulting in the crisis of the Great Depression. Attempts to solve the crisis through the arm of a managerial state proved ineffectual, and the crisis dragged itself out until the exogenous factor of the war created the conditions for a rather remarkable recovery and a rising rate of profit. Besides the recovery itself, the resolution to the crisis ushered in a new transformation in the international system: the realization of the US as a superpower, the central hegemon over the global economy. This had been planned prior to the entry of the US into the war,[30] and it quickly took steps to ensure this ascendency. International systems such as Bretton Woods were put into place, which created the International Monetary Fund, and the

International Bank for Reconstruction and Development (now the World Bank). This system also entailed the introduction of fixed exchange rates to facilitate global trade, with the US dollar serving as the international reserve currency; to increase confidence in the dollar, the currency was pegged to gold at $35 an ounce. These policies helped to integrate the world into a common economic system under the auspices of US leadership, and assisted in pushing forward the long postwar boom.

Breakdown

The forces that set off expansionary waves call into motion the forces that will inevitably undermine it and make it harder and harder to maintain a rising rate of profit. As long as Western Europe and Japan remained underdeveloped, the US could maintain its expansion. In terms of manufacturing exports, the US peaked as early as 1953, with its foreign-bound manufacturing output constituting 29.3% of total world exports.[31] Three years later this had fallen to 15%, and then to 18.7% in 1959. Percentage of total world manufacturing exports for the US would bottom out (in the context of the Fordist long wave) at 13.4% in 1971. This sharp decline reflected the recovery of the industrialized world and their increasing competitiveness in the global market: between 1953 and 1971 manufacturing exports from Japan grew from 2.8% to 10%, while exports from Germany rose from 9.7% to 15.4%. As foreign competition rose, the US rate of profit resettled into stagnation, peaking in 1965 and falling. Unemployment rose from a historic low of 2.9% in 1953 to 6.8% in 1958, though it would fall to 3.6% in 1968 – though the Vietnam War played a role in offsetting this decline in demand.

Throughout the postwar long boom the industrial cycles or Juglar waves continued. Accordingly, a minor recession occurred in 1957–1958; this was staved off by the application of Keynesian monetary policies (carried out by the Federal Reserve) and socially-oriented stimulus policies. These included the pumping of money into the economy to drive down interest rates and simultaneously increase inflation. Worried about changes in the dollar, European countries began to exchange their dollars for gold – significantly threatening the stability of the Bretton Woods system. In response, the Federal Reserve rose interest rates, effectively saving Bretton Woods and stabilizing the nascent system. On the international level, mechanisms such as the London Gold Pool were put into place that allowed the central banks of various countries to regulate the price of gold at the levels determined by Bretton Woods. Likewise, multilateral trade negotiations such as the Kennedy Round of the General Agreement on Trades and Tariffs sought to coordinate the free-trade activities of the dominant countries – with a predictably mixed set of results. Yet for the degree of coordination and organization taking place on an international level, there were definitive limitations to the postwar system that would quickly reveal themselves towards the latter part of the 1960s. As David Harvey writes:

...the period from 1965 to 1973 was one in which the inability of Fordism and Keynesianism to contain the inherent contradictions of capitalism became more and more apparent. On the surface, these difficulties could best be captured by one word: rigidity. There were problems with the rigidity of long-term and large-scale fixed capital investments in mass-production systems that precluded much flexibility of design and presumed stable growth in invariant consumer markets. There were problems of rigidities in the labour markets, and in labour contracts (especially in the so-called 'monopoly sector'... The rigidities of state commitments also became more serious as entitlement programs (social security, pension rights, etc.) grew under pressure to keep legitimacy at a time when rigidities in production restricted any expansion in the fiscal basis for state expenditures. The only tool of flexible response lay in monetary policy, in the capacity to print money at whatever rate appeared necessary to keep the economy stable. And so began the inflationary *wave that was eventually to sink the postwar boom.*[32]

In other words, the very structures that had accelerated the Fordist wave into prosperity proved incapable of reversing a falling rate of profit. This was exacerbated with wartime spending in Vietnam, which coupled with the expenditures necessary for President Johnson's Great Society program. Facing a money shortage, Johnson directed the Federal Reserve to print money detached from the gold supply. Had the economy been growing at a consistent rate, this increase in the money supply would have been without widespread effect. Because the rate of profit was falling, however, the entry of new money into circulation amplified inflation levels. In 1966 inflation stood at 2.86%, but increased at a steady rate annually, reaching 5.46% in 1969. The tension between the falling rate of profit and the increasing rate of inflation began, once again, to undermine the Bretton Woods system. Foreign governments rushed to exchange their dollars for gold, outstripping the available supply in the gold resources.

In 1971, West Germany officially exited Bretton Woods, precipitating a drastic decline in the value of the dollar. In response, Switzerland and France demanded to exchange their dollars for gold, further troubling the dollar. With the dollar falling, Switzerland followed West Germany's lead and exited Bretton Woods. These events occurred alongside a remarkably high unemployment rate (6.1%) and inflation rate (5.84%). The response would be the infamous "Nixon Shock": on August 31st, 1971, President Nixon directed the US Treasury to end the convertibility of the dollar into gold, formally ending the Bretton Woods arrangement and transforming fixed exchange rates into flexible ones. To combat inflation, an executive order was issued to impose a three-month wage and price control.

The Nixon Shock and the crisis it sought to manage signaled the end of the postwar long boom, and by extension the long wave that had been ushered in by the introduction of semi-automated mass-production techniques (Fordism). This crisis would continue on into the 1970s, described today as the era of "stagflation" – high unemployment and high inflation. As a result, standards of living fell across the US, compounded by the OPEC oil boycott of 1973, which set off a rise in fuel and transportation costs. As a result, the rate of profit continued to fall throughout the decade, with the industrial economy entering into long-term stagnation. As industry fell, however, a new sector of the economy was on the rise. This was the return of finance capital, which gained new traction with the ushering in of the post-Bretton Woods floating exchange rates by President Nixon. Thus what we have come to call "neoliberalism" can be said to start at this point, in the decline of the Fordist system; indeed, one of neoliberalism's most stalwart proponents, Chicago School economist Milton Friedman, had sent confidential memorandums to President Nixon urging him to abandon the Bretton Woods arrangement, noting that it would be a boom for finance capitalism.[33] It is by no accident that it was across this decade that what I call the "neoliberal-New Right opportunity structure" arose to take advantage of the crisis in order to implement a neoliberal policy regime. This topic will be taken up in Chapter 2.

Conditions of the New Long Wave

Neo-Schumpterians such as Perez and Freeman see the 1970s as the take-off of a new long wave, one based on the technological revolution of information-communication technologies (ICT) that had emerged from the military laboratories of World War II and slowly gained traction across the postwar boom. It is true that it was during the 1970s, with the introduction of the cheap microprocessor, that ICT began to integrate itself throughout industry and society. They became especially prominent in the trading floors of the newly-empowered financial exchanges, but ICT also found its application throughout industry, which streamlined much of Fordist semi-automation with new labor-saving technologies. Michael Roberts has shown that while the rate of profit fell across the 1970s the organic composition of capital rose (as expected); much of this can perhaps be attributed to higher degrees of technological integration in all aspects of life. It wouldn't be until well into the 1980s, however, that the wholesale adaptation of ICT would become commonplace.

At the same time, a series of other forces must be taken into account when considering the take-off of the new post-Fordist long wave. At the center of this effort is a series of measures to counter-act the falling rate of profit. The integration of ICT and other labor-saving technologies is central to this concern, but essentially every policy enacted from President Reagan onwards has made this its credo. It is only in this context that we can understand the sort of "race-to-the-bottom" economic and trade policies pursued from the 1980s onwards. One early example of this was the "Volcker Shock" of the early 80s, carried out by Reagan's Federal Reserve chairman Paul Volcker (himself retained from the Carter administration, having earlier helped orchestrate the Nixon Shock). In the Volcker Shock, interest rates were tripled in an attempt to cure stagflation. This policy not only increased significantly the burden of debts held by working-class families, pushing many into poverty; it also accelerated the de-industrialization of the US, triggering waves of factory closures and giving rise to what is called the "Rust Belt." This, in turn, pushed the direction of excess money supply from the investments into industry to investments in financial instruments, driving higher the financialization of the economy.

This shock occurred alongside attacks on organized labor and a cutting of taxes for the wealthiest of Americans. These conditions exacerbated the pauperization of the working class, but also precipitated a widespread transformation in the class makeup of the United States. As manufacturing employment stagnated, more and more workers were forced into low-wage service-sector jobs. The overall shift from a Keynesian demand-side policy regime to a neoliberal supply-side regime added a tendency towards wage stagnation in this dynamic transformation. During the Fordist postwar long boom, wages grew in accordance with the increasing levels of productivity; in the post-Fordist long wave, however, wages in the form of hourly compensation have increased by only 8.7% – the majority of which occurred between 1995 and 2002.[34] This has occurred despite a *growth in net productivity of 72.2% since the end of the long boom*. This indicates that the rate of exploitation has sped up considerably, extracting higher rates of surplus value from workers. The result has been a sharp increase in income inequality, with the top 10% of income earners taking a greater and greater share of the total US income and nearly rivaling that of the bottom 90%.

Throughout the period of 1983–2007, the gross domestic income (GDI) continued to rise, but the portion of this income realized in the form of wages and salaries paid to persons lagged behind, seeing only marginal gains. In 1983 the GDI stood at 14,590, with wages and salaries constituting 46.8% of this total. By 1997 the GDI had increased to 31,390, but income from wages and salaries constituted only a 45.1% share. The percentages continued to fall over the next decade; when the GDI reached 48,640 in 2007, wages and salary income held at 44.2%. Given this divergence, further reflected in the growing income gap, one might assume that the United States was heading towards an underconsumption crisis. In reality, quite the opposite was the case: consumer spending was *outpacing* the limitations of income. Despite the stagnation of wages (which becomes a decline in wages if inflation is taken into account), standards of living rose throughout this period. This is due to the rising role of debt to offset the elimination of workers and high wages from the productive sectors. In a windfall move for finance capitalism, "consumer credit" became the instrument of choice for trying to sustain the rate of profit, providing what appeared to be the supply-side alternative to Keynesian policies of full employment.

This debt takes on a variety of forms, from the extension of lines of credit for consumer goods to home loans to borrowed capital for investment purposes, either for productive investments or financial investments. This is part and parcel of the ongoing financialization of the economy that launched in this time period. Ultimately, what we're dealing with in this current long wave is the restructuring of capitalism as a whole. If the previous long wave was one built upon a productive infrastructure managed by industrial monopolies, we now exist in a productive infrastructure based on information technology, services, and finance. In short, the outcome of the crisis of the 1970s was a transition towards *post-Fordist neoliberalism.*

We should not take the term "post-Fordism" to entail the surpassing and elimination of Fordism, with its managerial perspective and regulation of the worker through the patterns of production. The deindustrialization in the United States was only made possible through a wider global restructuring, which pushed the Fordist mode of production into countries with low wages, low taxation rates, and low worker protections. The developing world thus becomes one, from the perspective of the developed world, of "peripheral Fordism." Far away and out of sight, these spaces of hyper-exploitation accelerate the production of goods whose consumer base isn't to be found amongst the workers who produce them; it is the populations of the deindustrialized, "developed" world who are the recipients. As John Smith writes:

> Export-oriented industrialization (or, from a northern perspective, "outsourcing") is the only capitalist option for poor countries not endowed with abundant natural resources. Under its aegis, the "developing nations' share of global manufactured exports rose

from around 5 percent in the pre-globalization period to close on 30 percent by the turn of the millennium, while the share of manufactured goods in the South's exports tripled in barely ten years, stabilizing in the early 1990s at more than 60 percent... In 1970, barely 10 percent of their manufactured imports came from what was then called the third world; by the turn of the millennium, this share—of a greatly expanded total—had quintupled.[35]

The transformation of the developing world into the production centers for the developed world has not been an organic process, but a consistent campaign of economic blackmail. During the 1960s the developing world, represented on the international stage through coalitions and groups such as the Non-Alignment Movement (left-leaning nations that sought independence from both US and Soviet hegemony) and the Group of 77 (organized by the United Nations Conference on Trade and Development in 1974) achieved growth through developmentalism, an attempt to balance the demands of international trade and foreign investment with the growth of domestic markets through protectionist measures. Support from developmentalism came from the developed world, with the Bretton Woods institutions of the IMF and World Bank providing loans to assist the process. The rates of growth appeared as outpacing the growth of debt – until, at least, the global decline of the 1970s. Debt levels steadily increased, becoming a crisis during the Volcker Shock. It was at this point that an ideologically reformed IMF and World Bank (discussed in Chapter 2) offered neoliberalism in exchange for debt relief; developmentalism would be dismantled through deregulation, privatization, and the removal of trade barriers. Instead of nurturing domestic industry and consumer bases, the widespread utilization of "special economic zones" allows corporations to set up shop in host countries for a fraction of the costs associated with the developed world. At one time the north–south divide described the relationship between imperialist countries and their subjugated colonies; today, this continues in the form of the divide between post-Fordism and Fordism, between the owners of capital and the consumers of production and the workforce.

For Ernest Mandel, the current long wave is one dominated by stagnation, an argument that gels with what we saw earlier regarding the falling rate of profit.[36] Each of these attempts – financialization, the shift of production to the global south, the rigorous assault on labor, the deconstructions of trade barriers and economic regulation at home and abroad – is a clear indication of a resolution to this wider, protracted crisis. Since the early 1980s, we've witnessed a general speed-up, on a global level, of the rate of exploitation and an accelerated shift from what Marx would describe as the productive sectors to the unproductive sectors. With these conditions in mind, we can turn now to the Great Recession.

The Great Recession and Beyond

Systemic

The inauguration of the neoliberal period was heralded as the coming of a "New Economy," one freed from the ups and downs of business cycles and the inflexibility of the old industrial economy. In the New Economy, information technology would take center-stage, with investors and venture capitalists poised to reap high returns from pouring capital into tech start-ups. Service-sector employment and the proliferation of what some have referred to as "immaterial labor"[37] were to lend a newfound flexibility to the labor pool, opening the space for people to have a greater say in defining their lives. The New Economy was one of "creative capitalism," in which the old borders were broken down and everything was suddenly capable of being realized on a global level. Underneath the utopian veneer, however, the stagnation remained, its existence obscured by a rising tide of debt and a population being made less creative and free, but more precarious and restrained.

Key to the obscuring of the actual conditions of the economy were the policies maintained by the Federal Reserve throughout the 1990s. Interest rates were kept relatively low, encouraging the spreading of debt in the general population and speculative activities on the behalf of the finance capitalists. Enthused on the apparent unending source of high returns from ICT firms, a bubble began to grow in the mid-90s, the existence of which went unnoticed; in many cases, capital flowed straight into firms when they did as little as add "e-" or ".com" to their names – a practice referred to by some as "prefix-investing". This was the growth of the Dotcom Bubble, which finally burst in 2000. Stocks, which had soared during the course of the bubble, crashed, leading many firms to simply close up shop and many others to lose heavy portions of their market capitalizations. The "get-big-fast" mentality that had expanded the bubble had quickly run into structural limitations: ICT firms needed to have a continually expanding consumer base, which in turn pivoted on dual needs of high demand for information technology and the physical infrastructure to support it. The wave of speculation, in other words, had pushed supply to outpace demand in an environment where demand itself could not be organically fostered due to uneven development. The bursting of the Dotcom Bubble was reflective of an underlying tension that was present in the conditions of the new long wave – not unlike the uneven development that had contributed so much to the Great Depression.

The damage wrought by the burst of the Dotcom Bubble was amplified by the attacks of September 11th, 2001, with the two effectively ushering in the early 2000s recession. By the end of 2001, job losses were recorded at 1.735 million, with a multi-quarter fall in the rate of GDP growth. The fear of a "lost decade" of stagnant growth similar to that of Japan resonated throughout Washington and Wall Street, prompting the Federal Reserve, under the leadership of Alan Greenspan, to double-down on the Fed policies of the 90s: interest rates were pushed down from 6.5% to a historic low of 1% to encourage lending, and by extension, growth. Greenspan's policies would have, however, an unintended consequence. In the late 90s, increasing returns in real-estate investment and housing sales had led many to begin to take on mortgages. With interest rates at 1%, the rate of mortgages accelerated exorbitantly, leading to higher and higher housing prices (a 15% increase would occur by 2005). This, in turn, attracted more to turn to the housing market as an opportunity for investment. Large portions of consumer purchasing power became powered by still higher levels of debt, as individuals began to engage in mortgage-based debt re-financing to take on more loans, operating on the anticipation of high returns through housing sales.

The enthusiasm that drove up the Housing Bubble, in other words, differed very little from the enthusiasm that drove up the Dotcom Bubble. And just as with the Dotcom Bubble, the Housing Bubble exhibited a complete detachment from the material conditions of the real economy. Unlike its predecessor, the Housing Bubble posed an existential risk to the entirety of monopoly-finance capitalism, and with it, the entirety of the US economy. This was because the deregulated environment allowed lenders to engage in predatory lending practices; high-risk loans were in turn bundled as securities to be bought and sold in the finance market to open up more capital for lending. These securities, in turn, proliferated through a finance market that was becoming increasingly centralized as firms consolidated into larger and larger monopolies. This vast and interwoven structure rested itself on an ever-expanding bubble that had seen investments double from nearly $300 billion in 1989 to $600 billion by the mid-2000s. Monopoly-finance capital, in other words, was a house of cards.

This house of cards is what toppled over in the beginning of the Great Recession. It's easy to look at this shortened and condensed scenario and immediately point fingers at multiple factors. It was the Federal Reserve's involvement in interest rates, one might say, or it was the fault of the deregulatory environment that allowed the investment banks and other lenders to take advantage of would-be home owners and transform their debt into a tradeable commodity. Others might point to the people who took out the loans in the first place, accruing debt that was unsustainable. Each of these points have merit, and none can be fully isolated from one another. The Federal Reserve *was* compelled to hold down interest rates to avoid long-term stagnation, precisely because of uneven development in the "installation" of the new long wave. The banks engaged in their practices *because* it is the nature of the neoliberal epoch, wholly concerned with amplifying profits after the crisis of the 1970s. And people *were* driven to turn to debt to sustain themselves, as the traditional means for accumulating wealth. The Great Recession, in other words, was not about bad banking, moral hazards, or irrational behavior; it can be contextualized as the coming-together of multiple systemic tendencies inherent to this phase of the system's development. Profitability had been reduced to a gambling that took place far from any visibility, as the 2011 report of the Financial Crisis Inquiry Commission reported:

> *In the years leading up to the crisis, too many financial institutions, as well as too many households, borrowed to the hilt, leaving them vulnerable to financial distress or ruin if the value of their investments declined even modestly. For example, as of 2007, the five major investment banks—Bear Stearns, Goldman Sachs, Lehman Brothers, Merrill Lynch, and Morgan Stanley—were operating with extraordinarily thin capital. By one measure, their leverage ratios were as high as 40 to 1, meaning for every $40 in assets, there was only 1$ in capital to cover losses. Less than a 3$ drop in asset values*

could wipe out a firm. To make matters worse, much of their borrowing was short-term, in the overnight market — meaning the borrowing had to be renewed each and every day. For example, at the end of 2007, Bear Stearns had $11.8 billion in equity and $383.6 billion in liabilities and was borrowing as much as $70 billion in the overnight market. It was the equivalent of a small business with $50.000 in equity borrowing $1.6 million, with $296,750 of that due each and every day. One can't really ask, "What were they thinking?" when it seems that too many of them were thinking alike. And the leverage was often hidden — in derivatives positions, in off-balance-sheet entities, and through "window dressing" of financial reports available to the investing public.[38]

What's Next?

Since the onslaught of the Great Recession, global central banks have coordinated their actions in order to try to revive the slumping global economy. Part and parcel of this effort has been the further holding down of interest rates in accordance with a program of quantitative easing. The other aspect was the pumping of cash into the economy, which between 2009 and 2015 would reach upwards of some $12 trillion. Despite these efforts, the recovery from the recession appears to have fallen short of expectations. In the United States, for example, there appeared to have been a multiyear jobless recovery (this was, in fact, the third jobless recovery of the neoliberal period, following the 1990 recession and the early 2000s recession).[39] While there is evidence to suggest that by 2015 this tide was turning, the duration of upturn lasted much longer than other recessions in modern history. Indeed, GDP growth in multiple regions grew at a slow pace against the expectations of a sharp rebound: China's rate of growth declined from 10% in 2011 to 7% in 2014, while Europe's GDP growth fell by 10% below average and the US's GDP growth has grown only 20% over 2009 levels.[40] Effects in other regions varied, indicating that as a whole the recovery has unfolded in an uneven manner. By 2016 the IMF was revising its global growth forecasts to negative after several years of positive outlook, citing an increasingly unstable economic and political environment.[41] In a similar vein, the Bank for International Settlements issued a statement that the global slowdown – led primarily by China, but also by a questionable stock market in the US – threatened to generate widespread economic turbulence.[42] And finally the Brookings Institute's TIGER index (that is, the "tracking index for global recovery") found as early as October 2015 that the "world economy is beset by a dangerous combination of divergent growth patterns, deficient demand, and deflationary risks. While growth prospects for the advanced economies have improved, emerging market economies are now leading the world economy into a slump."[43]

The irony is that this specter of turbulence – and the sluggish recovery as a whole – has occurred despite not only the pumping of trillions of dollars into the global economy but also a mounting wall of cash held by corporations. The balance sheets of corporations had escalated so much in the years following the Great Recession that Bain Capital in 2012 announced that "global capital had swollen to some $600 trillion".[44] The world, in other words, was caught in a situation where money itself was overabundant – which, as Bain is quick to remind us, is not necessarily a good thing. In 2014, economist Daniel Altman noted in *Foreign Policy* that "20 percent of capital in the world's two biggest economies may well be sitting idle. If distributed evenly, this would mean one out of every five computers, machines, and vehicles involved in production at every American and European business would be doing nothing."[45]

This may look like the scenario that Baran and Sweezy laid out in *Monopoly Capital*, where monopolistic corporations accumulate surplus to the point where it can no longer be fully reabsorbed, and effectively become capital sinks that tend to stagnate in the long run. But as we saw earlier, the problem with Baran and

Sweezy's assessment was that it was relative to their place and time, and mistook the material conditions of their moment for a long-term tendency in capitalist development. Their theory disputed the perspective of the economists and researchers included towards long-wave analysis, yet in historical retrospection it seems clear that the shock of innovation, alongside the spatial reorganization of capitalist accumulation on a global level, could open up spaces for the absorption of capital. Counter-acting tendencies, in other words, were still capable of staving off endemic threats to the capitalist system.

The question here then becomes one of innovation. Following the long-wave theories of neo-Schumpeterians such as Perez, the crisis of the Great Recession should mark a turning point in the current "techno-economic paradigm" (i.e. the neoliberal era). The unevenness of the installation stage should be smoothed out, and a new onslaught of innovations pooled during the downturn should be primed to take off. Baran and Sweezy's perspective would prove true in the event that no significant innovations accumulated, yet this hardly seems the case: in the years during and immediately following the Recession, advancements in information technology (namely, the so-called "internet-of-things" technology) and green technology have attracted significant buzz. Smart cities based on sustainable energy practices and the networking together of digital communication platforms into a multi-scaled mesh became the promised city of tomorrow; driverless cars, automated factories, new forms of agriculture, cutting-edge recycling techniques, so on and so forth, grace headlines on a nearly daily basis. The encounter of the green and the communicative, against the backdrop of mounting corporate balance sheets, appears to be poised to mark a post-Recession "golden age" (to borrow from Perez's parlance) – yet by and large, this picture does not seem to be something that is actually being realized.

There are multiple dimensions to this problem. One of these is the problem of job growth, itself as essential to overall economic growth. As briefly mentioned above, it took some six years for employment rates to reach pre-recession levels – yet behind the surface statistics one finds a reality in which high-wage jobs are not being recovered at the pace of low-wage jobs, indicating that many displaced in the onset of the Great Recession are returning to the labor force worse off than they were before. This tendency, of course, existed *prior* to the Great Recession and has been the hallmark of the neoliberal era, having to do not only with the relocation of manufacturing elsewhere in the world but also the dynamics of job creation in an evolving market. In 1962, for example, the top five corporations in terms of market capitalization were AT&T, GM, Exxon, Dupont, and IBM. Each maintained a sizeable workforce: AT&T had 564,000 employees, GM had 605,000, Exxon had 150,000, Dupont had 101,000, and IBM had 81,000. In 2012, by contrast, this picture had radically altered, with the top five corporations being Apple, Exxon, Microsoft, Google, and Walmart. Each of these corporations maintain a significantly smaller workforce (with the exception of Walmart, the lowest-paying employer on the list): Apple's employees topped out at 76,000, Exxon at 77,000, Microsoft at 94,000, Google at 54,000, and Walmart at 2,200,000.[46]

According to the Brookings Institution, the time of the large monopoly corporation that dominated the Fordist era is changing – though it may not be over in the sense that advocates of the New Economy argued for in the 1990s. For the Brookings Institution, the tendency is one towards a declining need for labor, which becomes foregrounded as technology radically transforms the necessities of business. This is not only true for the established firm, but up-and-coming businesses such as start-ups. President Obama's 2012 Jumpstart Our Business Startups (JOBS) Act hoped to use small businesses as a pathway to growth through removing the barriers that prohibited entrepreneurs from going public – yet as the Brooking Institution's report points out, "companies going public often have relatively microscopic employment, particularly in high tech."[47] This is particularly true in regards to biotechnology, one of the fields assumed by Perez to be an engine of growth during the next stage of our current long wave; to quote Brookings again, "the median [biotechnology] firm that went public after 2000 had 49 employees in 2013, and all of them put together (roughly 100) had fewer than 8,000 employees in total. Moreover, more than 90 percent of these firms had no profits."[48] In the "cleantech" and green industry sectors there appear to be mixed signals: according to a 2012 study by the Bureau of Labor Statistics, "green jobs" were growing at a faster rate than other sectors, with some 20.4% of these jobs going to manufacturing.[49] In 2013, 78,000 green-energy jobs were added, but in the following year this dropped to 47,000.[50] For *Fortune*, the sharp decline in job growth was political in origin, as infighting over "every energy-related public policy question has created 'a climate of uncertainty that casts a cloud over clean energy industries'." Despite the undeniable role of exogenous factors such as these, there is an overarching trend that exists regardless of how we cut it, the reshuffling of labor allocation across the US points to a central aspect of Marx's theory of the TRPF: that variable capital will decline, raising the specter of a general crisis of profitability through the loss of value added. This is precisely why the entire political response to the Great Recession (discussed in Chapter 2) can appear as simply a return to the conditions that created the recession in the first place. As Kevin Carson succinctly describes:

> Conventional left-Keynesian economists are at a loss to imagine some basis on which a post-bubble economy can ever be re-established with anything like current levels of output and employment. This is especially unfortunate, given the focus of the Bush and Obama administration's banking policies on restoring asset prices to something approaching their pre-collapse value, and their economic

policies on at least partially reinflating the bubble economy as a
source of purchasing power...[51]

Thus the most fervent supporters of the Washington Consensus came to be befuddled when the economy didn't spring right back into action as anticipated. In 2015 Ben Bernanke, former Federal Reserve chief during the recession years, expounded an idea he had first seized upon in 2005 – that low demand was triggering a "savings glut" that was prohibiting growth.[52] The observation made by Bain Capital – that the world is "awash in capital" – seems to support this, yet it is certainly not the complete picture. As Michael Roberts has illustrated, the "cash walls" supposedly being hoarded by corporations are not idle, but flowing back into the finance sector, finding their realization as stocks, bonds, insurance, and the like.[53] Thus we are right back where we were before the economic conditions of the present long-wave bottomed out: high uneven development, high inequality, low investment in the "material economy" of production, and increasing rates of capital entering into the "immaterial" economy of finance. Bernanke should not be surprised at this state of affairs, for it is the natural result of policies that he himself helped construct!

Thus it appears that attempts at carrying out a successful institutional adaptation are being bypassed, with a turning point that does not turn at all. A successful deployment – with a corollary rise in the rate of profit – would require (at the very least): 1) the directing of capital away from the financial sector into constructive investments, particularly those in new innovations that pooled during the crisis; and 2) positive job growth and job mobility, to shrink the reserve army of the unemployed and to boost aggregate demand. The latter is beholden partially to the former (investments are necessary for the expansion of jobs available), but is also beholden to the nature of technological innovation itself. In an era of a rising organic composition of capital, embodied in the forms of increasing industrial automation and lean models of firms (as well as distributed manufacturing techniques proliferating on a localized scale), the need for skilled and unskilled labor decreases with each passing year, with no apparent outlet for this expanding reserve army. What this means is that even if the river of capital reversed from finance to investments, *there is no guarantee that it will boost the economy to the levels enjoyed, however prematurely, in the years prior to the Great Recession.* Setting into a lower equilibrium of supply and demand, prices and wages may very well be the natural outcome, but it is an outcome that the neoliberal structure is not equipped to handle.

Based on these factors, it is no exaggeration to say that neoliberalism itself is splitting apart. If the path of industrial policy, with the direction of capital into constructive investments with the aid of the state, comes to fruition, then we would declare that neoliberalism had formally ended. If the current path is pursued, then a return to recession conditions is extremely likely – and after a second round, it seems plausible that for even its most ardent supporters, neoliberalism will appear to have overstayed its welcome. If we transition to a different set of expectations of what we want and get from the economy, that too closes the door on the dominant ideologies of our time. The problem arises, however, when we stop to consider that neoliberalism is not simply an economic paradigm, but a political one as well. A crisis in the economic dimensions of neoliberalism and an uncertain outlook for its future would inherently entail a crisis in its political dimensions. We will now turn to the political history of neoliberalism and demonstrate that this is precisely the case.

Chapter 2

The Rise and Breakdown of the Neoliberal Establishment

What Is Neoliberalism?

How are we to properly define neoliberalism? Perhaps the simplest way is the best: for Johanna Brockman, neoliberalism constitutes "a set of ideas about how to organize markets, states, enterprises, and populations, which shape government policies."[1] Continuing, she suggests that these policy sets "include deregulation, liberalization of trade and capital flows, anti-inflationary stabilization, and privatization of state enterprises." Her assessment of neoliberalism as an explicitly political program dovetails closely with Michel Foucault's own early analysis of the economic paradigm, which stressed the way in which neoliberal economists sought to find the ideal arrangement of policies that could aid and accelerate the growth of markets.[2] Foucault came to situate the bulk of his concerns then on the state itself – a move that is absolutely important as we will see over the course of this chapter. His approach, however, obscures a counter-tendency that threatens to undermine his analysis: as much as neoliberalism is about organizing markets, neoliberalism is also about making the market the de-facto organizing principle for the state and society. Foucault recognizes this, but by ending his analysis at the state, he misses out on the way that these policy sets – or, more properly, this *policy regime* – emerges not from the state as an autonomous actor, but from the state serving as the *hegemonic mechanism* of the ruling class.

It is in the works of Antonio Gramsci that one will find a theory of how hegemonic mechanisms function in capitalist society; after all, his definition of the word entailed the subordination of certain social groups and classes by a ruling class.[3] While many would focus on power in its violent dimensions, Gramsci's hegemony emphasized the far more subtle systems at work, particularly through the ways in which intellectual consensus is mobilized via the integration of class interest, media, and the state. It wouldn't be until the path-breaking socio-logical work of C. Wright Mills and G. William Domhoff, however, that tools were crafted to display the ways in which class power operates through individuals and institutions to move the state, at both local and national levels, to their own ends.[4] This "elite theory," as it has been called, draws our attention to two intertwining phenomena: the way in which class power operates as a kind of loose network structure, and the way the shifts in the dominant power can be traced to the ascendency of a given "faction" of the ruling class over another faction. Domhoff's work is extremely provocative in this regard, clearly illustrating how throughout modern history, for example, factions whose business interests are more nationally-oriented in outlook will compete for a policy regime that privileges themselves at the expense of internationally-oriented business and vice versa.

If neoliberalism can be articulated as a hegemonic function with a specific historical context, it would follow that evidence of a changing make-up in the arrangement of class power could be detected. As reviewed in the previous chapter, neoliberalism not only emerged in the general crisis of Keynesianism across the 1970s, but marked a fundamental shift from an economy dominated by monopoly-industrial capital to one dominated by monopoly-financial capital. This is not to say, of course, that finance did not play an important role in the Keynesian era (or that industrial capitalism is irrelevant in the neoliberal era). What this means more properly is that the role played by finance capital *supersedes and subordinates* the role of industrial capital. This hegemony of finance capitalism is not a new development in the history of capitalism (though its current global scope is indeed unprecedented): the early 1900s saw a similar growth of financial monopolies, leading non-Marxist economists such as Thorstein Veblen and J.A. Hobson (alongside Marxist thinkers including Rudolf Hilferding and Vladimir Lenin) to conclude that the tension between finance and industry would destabilize the economy as a whole.

In the wake of the Great Depression, the US government took extensive measures to reign in the excesses of financial capitalism, launching in 1932 an investigation into the banking sector. What they uncovered was the power of the financial capitalist class, represented by a network of individuals and interlocking corporate directorships – in other words, they honed in on the locus of finance's hegemonic function. From this investigation emerged the famed Glass-Steagal Act and the Securities and Exchange Commission (SEC), both of which served to break the back of finance capitalism's power and assisted in the transition towards what would become the postwar Keynesian hegemony. It is by no mistake, then, that in the neoliberal era Glass-Steagal was repealed (carried out by President Bill Clinton and a Treasury Department led by a former Goldman Sachs executive) and the SEC has become increasingly lax in its regulatory enforcement. It is also no mistake that this period has seen an enormous accumulation of wealth in the financial class: in 1982, the FIRE industries (finance, insurance, and real estate) were the source of wealth for only 24% of the *Forbes* Fortune 400, with finance alone only encompassing 9%. By 2007, FIRE represented 34% of Fortune 400 wealth, with finance making up the bulk of this at 27.3%. Manufacturing, which stood at 15.3% in 1982, dropped to 9.5% in 2007. Similarly, at the end of the 1980s, the top ten of the nation's executive compensation did not include any from the financial sector; by 2007 this scenario was reversed with four out of the five top-earning executives coming from finance.[5]

It would be mistaken, however, to say that neoliberalism, as both an economic organization (in terms of the relationship between the market and society) and a hegemonic mechanism (in terms of the relationship between class power and the state), can be strictly equalized with the dominance of monopoly-finance capitalism. Instead, we should view this transformation as a trend organic to capitalism itself. In each aspect of the neoliberal policy regime – the removal of regulatory controls, the attacks on deregulation, the explosion of power and wealth in the financial sector, the shifting of manufacturing to the so-called "developing world," so on and so forth – we can see a movement to increase the wealth of the capitalist class no matter what the cost. As we saw in the previous chapter, capitalism appears to be exhibiting what Marx anticipated: the rate of the tendency of the profit to fall. Each set of policies carried out by the state appears, from this perspective, as something completely and utterly predictable, as a response to the increased difficulty of continuing the momentum of growth. Indeed, Giovanni Arrighi in his book *The Long Twentieth Century* notes the uncanny resemblance between the current moment and cycles of economic crisis going back to the 1400s.[6] In each cycle, the financialization of the dominant country's economy has resulted from an increasing difficulty of extracting profits in the context of overarching stagnation. Furthermore, Arrighi depicts each acceleration of finance as corresponding to the "terminal crisis" for each dominant national-economic hegemony. Neoliberalism, in other words, may not be the sign of strength and prosperity that its adherents claim it to be, but a symptom of an irreversible decline.

If evidence of this decline can be found in economic tendencies (which, as we argued in the previous chapter, is the case), there should be similar evidence to be found in the hegemonic mechanism of the state. There is good reason to see that this is precisely the case: the 2016 election cycle has seen the remarkable rise of economic populisms, both left-wing and right-wing, that bitterly contest the neoliberal consensus inscribed into the heart of each of their respective party's establishments. Both have been able to mobilize support from large portions of the population, indicating a significant disenfranchisement with "business-as-usual" politics and economics. Both appealed to the working class – the class hit hardest by the neoliberal policy regime – and both reject many of the tenets of the globalization of trade and the financialization of the economy while also supporting a regeneration of the American manufacturing economy. The difference is that one side sees the necessity of returning to the policy regime of the Keynesian "golden age" of capitalism, while the other appeals to future "golden age" based on nationalism and strength. In each case, the neoliberals in each party establishment have mounted vigorous defenses of themselves, in a gambit to maintain the policy regime of the current era as far as it can go. In order to truly grasp the significance of this breakdown of political consensus on the national stage, we must review this instance in the context of neoliberalism's trajectory through the American political system – and it is to this that we now turn.

From the Margins to Consensus

The pivot from a quasi-Keynesian consensus to the current neoliberal consensus, unfolding across nearly half a century, has been contingent upon what Sara Diamond has referred to as a "domestic and international political opportunity structure."[7] This opportunity structure, the foundation upon which the new hegemony has been constructed, requires "(1) increased corporate funding; (2) accelerated organizational development; and (3) incipient mobilization on an expanded issues agenda."[8] It operates, in other words, as a well-oiled machine reflecting the interests of certain sectors of the capitalist class while simultaneously operating as a nebulous social movement aimed at fundamentally transforming the functioning of formal and informal methods of governance. Through it the citizenry is mobilized on a grassroots level to demand certain reforms or propel new political candidates into office; think-tanks are established to provide education to the public and the political classes; experts are provided to serve in the middle levels of government, advise the upper echelons of government, author textbooks, and act as pundits for the media. Most importantly, for the sake of its own success, it has managed to bring together issues often seen as connected only disparately in the eyes of the electorate. Diamond's own detailed analysis of this political opportunity structure focuses primarily on socially conservative, nationalistic, and foreign policy-oriented networks; in our brief overview here, we will focus on the more distinctively economic-oriented networks (though it must be pointed out that, historically, these networks have been conjoined at the hip).

While neoliberalism itself has multiple points of origin, the most obvious bedrock was the early theories of Austrian School economists Ludwig von Mises and F.A. Hayek, whose writings in the first half of the 1900s argued for the inability of economic planning, the universality of the market's "self-organizing" nature, the primacy of price signals, and above all, the role of competition as a rational regulatory mechanism for society as a whole. This primary goal of the Austrian economic vision was one in which markets would be *dis-embedded* from social regulation (traditionally carried out by the state apparatus), and would in turn embed social relations within its own matrices of relations.[9] While von Mises, Hayek, and their colleagues fancied themselves the inheritors of a *laissez-faire* tradition stretching back to J.B. Say's interpretation of Adam Smith (addressed briefly in the previous chapter), their writings must be contextualized in their historical moment: the rise of the Soviet Union in Russia, and the creation of "Red Vienna" under the city's social-democratic municipal government. Both von Mises and Hayek could be counted amongst "the remnants of old Vienna's privileged urban elites whose security had been shattered, whose savings had been decimated by wartime and postwar inflation, and whose taxes were financing the pioneering housing programs of Vienna's socialist municipal administration."[10]

The rise of forces sympathetic to the Soviet project, and perhaps the more prominent popularity of managerial economies in the Western world (taking, at various points, Keynesian, Institutionalist, social-democratic and even socialist directions) posed significant barriers to propagation of the Austrian's proto-neoliberal ideals. By the 1930s, however, a transnational network began to form that would contain the seeds of the neoliberal synthesis. The first evidence of this was the Walter Lippman Colloquium, held in France in 1939, with attendees including von Mises, Hayek, and members of the German Freiburg School of economics. It was here that the nature of the neoliberal market economy was hypothesized, with the attendees coming to the conclusion that while market competition would serve as an idealized regulatory of social activity, it required at the minimum "an active and extremely vigilant policy" – in other words, a state apparatus tooled towards ensuring the market's regulation of society.[11] This entails not so much a state that actively intervenes in the market at the functional level (in the form of say, Keynesian macroeconomic policy), but a state whose strategic interventions operate through generating conditions equitable for market functioning.

This synthesis suffered a setback during the Second World War and the postwar recovery, as state-managed markets and strong labor policies came to be the dominant norm for economic development. In response, Hayek in 1945 launched the Mont Pelerin Society (MPS), a neoliberal "thought collective" that would allow free-market economists, philosophers, and social scientists to develop a long-term agenda for neoliberal alternatives to the Keynesian orthodoxy. The goal, he wrote, was "to enlist the support of the best minds in formulating a programme which has a chance of gaining general support."[12] Very quickly, the MPS was to develop ties with American think-tanks and organizations that were pro-business and anti-New Deal – including the National Association of Manufacturers, the Foundation for Economic Education and the American Enterprise Association (which would soon change its name to the American Enterprise Institute). In England, the MPS's Antony Fisher established the Institute of Economic Affairs (IEA), which sought to strengthen ties with the British Conservative Party. These multiple poles of national and transnational integration would serve as the key pillars in the development of the opportunity structure as the crisis of the 1970s came into view.

It is worth pointing out that the ideology of neoliberalism developed within the MPS was never a singular one, but a synthesis that operated at the level of a consensus that moved in sometimes contradictory directions. The Austrian contingency, represented by Hayek and his followers, at once overlapped and diverged with the presence of Chicago School economists, represented primarily by Milton Friedman. While Friedman and Hayek were indeed close colleagues, the difference in their overall economic philosophies produced two distinctive approaches. For the Austrians, the focus would come to be on the rule of law, in keeping with the early neoliberal imperative of constructing market-optimized governance (the MPS, in fact, would open an office in the University of Chicago's Law School); for the Chicago monetarists, on the other hand, the political process itself was to be treated the same as the market – the "flat ontology of the neoclassical model of the economy."[13] This distinction produced two different forms of anti-statism, the tension between which we can perhaps use as the measure of what precisely neoliberal rationality entails: at one end we have the optimization of market action through particular sets of juridical constructs, and on the other end, the competitive organi-

zation of the market itself serving as a sort of informal methodology for "law and order." Insofar as the state has a role for
Chicago School economists like Friedman, it is through monetary
policy carried out by governments and central banks to "ensure a
constant and predictable level of monetary growth to 'provide a
stable background for the economy.'"[14]

During the 1950s and 60s the MPS and the Chicago School, as
well as connected organizations such as the Foundation for
Economic Education (FEE) and the American Enterprise Institute
(AEI), enjoyed funding and promotion from the conservative
business elite, with many of their targets of critique dovetailing
the interests of these very same benefactors. These included the
post-New Deal welfare programs, tax rates, the power of trade
unions, international trade policy, and the role of corporate
monopolies in the economy.[15] At the same time, these ideas
remained rather marginal in the context of the postwar boom,
which appeared as having preemptively disproved everything
that the MPS and its extended network were advocating. When
the crisis of the 1970s struck, however, the *laissez-faire* ideology
that had been pieced together appeared to be taking on a new
relevance. As inflation turned into stagflation, the conservative
elite minority found their numbers boosted by a broader "right-
turn" in business outlook. Already entrenched right-wing philanthropies representing the interests of the conservative elite, such
as the Scaife, Bradley, Olin, Coors, and Koch Foundations, were
joined by a rising tide of new philanthropies as well as individual
corporate donors who pumped millions upon millions into both
socially and fiscally conservative organizations and
movements.[16]

This infusion of money boosted the standing of the fledgling
neoliberal movement. Most notably, the AEI quickly rose to
prominence and became the defining organ of the New Right
synthesis of social conservatism, hawkishness in foreign policy,
and neoliberalism in economic and monetary policy. In 1973, Paul

Weyrich and Edwin Feulner (himself a member of the MPS) secured funding from the Coors Foundation and the Scaife Foundation to launch the Heritage Foundation, a policy-influencing think-tank that sought to "unite conservatives from all of the different strands of the movement, the libertarians, neoconservatives, the religious and Christian conservatives, and traditional conservatives..."[17] A complimentary organization was the Cato Institute, launched by Ed Crane with money from Charles Koch – a conservative booster and MPS member. Both Hayek and Friedman would work very closely with Cato, while Crane himself moved the organization into alignment with the Atlas Foundation, a sort of "umbrella" for MPS-connected think-tanks launched by Antony Fisher. Each of these organizations were joined by a slew of other nationally-based, internationally-oriented think-tanks: the Manhattan Institute for Policy Research (based in New York City), the Fraser Institute (based in Ontario), the Pacific Research Institute (based in San Francisco), the Adam Smith Institute (based in London), the National Center for Policy Analysis, among others. Each of these were launched with close relations to one another (ties that continue to exist to this day), often sharing the same experts and figureheads, the same funding sources (the Scaife, Bradley, Olin, Coors, and Koch Foundations), and promoting the same deregulatory, anti-labor, anti-tax, anti-welfare pro-market perspectives espoused by the leading lights of the MPS – Hayek and Friedman.

The Reagan Revolution

While neoliberal monetarist policies found their first real applications under President Jimmy Carter, it was the ushering in of the "Reagan Revolution" that marked the breakthrough of the neoliberal mode of capitalism and the victory of the neoliberal-New Right opportunity structure. Many of the key principles in "Reaganomics" – tax reductions for the wealthy, deregulation,

Chicago-style monetary policy, etc. – were set down in a report of policy recommendations made by the Republican Study Committee; the authors of this paper, itself drafted under the watchful eye of the Heritage Foundation's Edwin Feulner, were in frequent contact with Hayek and Friedman, and summaries of the duo's economic theories were presented in the final draft.[18] Likewise, on the eve of the Reagan presidency the Heritage Foundation issued its thousand-paged *Mandate for Leadership: Policy Management in a Conservative Administration*, the recommendations of which mirrored those of the earlier Republican Study Committee. According to the Heritage Foundation, Reagan would ultimately implement some two-thirds of these recommended policies. The Hoover Institution, another organization in the neoliberal-New Right opportunity structure, published *The United States in the 1980s*, which also reinforced the neoliberal perspective for the Reagan era through essays written by Friedman and other Chicago School-affiliated economists.

Within the Reagan administration, the bulk of his economic team was drawn from the ranks of the neoliberals. Half of the president's Economic Advisory Board – defined by one Reagan adviser as the "board of directors for the development of Reaganomics"[19] – were Chicago School economists, with Friedman claiming the title of the "President's favorite." It's not hard to find the imprint of the MPS perspective on the majority of the president's early moves, from the infamous Volcker Shock to the brutal assault on organized labor during the ill-fated air-traffic controllers' strike to the slashing of government funding (aside from defense) to the privatization of welfare functions such as federally-subsidized housing for low-income families. Likewise, disastrous programs like the "enterprise zones" for urban development (that is, zones of low taxation and regulation to better the movement of capital) were drawn directly from the suggestions of thinkers like Hayek and organizations such as the Heritage Foundation. In each case, we can see clearly how the

Reagan administration set out to fulfill the desires of both the proto-neoliberals and the neoliberals – the reconfiguration of government, and the rationality of governance, towards a policy regime that enables the market to rise as the key regulator and mediator of social relations. While the term "trickle-down economics," proposed as an easy way to describe this new "supply-side" order, was meant to illustrate the self-organizing capabilities of the market, it also plays the role of the signifier for an entirely new set of social, political, and economic relations.

The influence of Reagan's economic agenda did not stop at the border, and sought to extend itself across the globe. In the first year of his presidency, Reagan considered withdrawing funding from the International Monetary Fund (IMF), a move that would have struck a near death-blow to the organization. In response, the IMF leadership purged from its ranks the Keynesian econo-mists who had been the drivers of the organization's agenda since its creation, and adopted the "structural adjustment program" (SAP) as its primary intervention technique.[20] The concept of the SAP was wholly in line with the neoliberal agenda, offering financial aid in exchange for privatization of public services, the removal of protectionist trade restrictions, tax cuts, and the selling off of state-owned assets. Following suit, the World Bank reshuffled its economics division, removing those who were sympathetic to Keynesian economics and replacing them with economists who operated in the Chicago School tradition.[21] Like the IMF, the World Bank adopted the SAP as a model for enforcing economic development in neoliberal parameters. In 1982, the IMF and World Bank were granted full authority to negotiate debt-relief programs for countries ensnared in the Third World debt crisis (which, as we may recall from the previous chapter, occurred at the hands of the Reagan adminis-tration through the Volcker Shock). This meant that the SAP would quickly be applied around the world, effectively cementing in place the neoliberalization of the global economic system – and by extension, the role of the United States at the helm of this system.

The neoliberalization of the United States was matched by the neoliberalization of Great Britain under Margaret Thatcher. Just as Reagan had drawn from the American pole of the neoliberal-New Right opportunity structure, the set of governmental protocols that constituted Thatcherism emerge from the British free-market think-tanks organized by MPS members – the Institute for Economic Affairs, the Adam Smith Institute and the Centre for Policy Studies, namely. Like Reagonomics, the British interpretation of neoliberalism was contingent on turning governmental structures over to the rationality of the market. Protectionist trade policies, which had incubated nationalized industries, were removed, triggering an influx of foreign capital that wore down the country's manufacturing base. Tax cuts and the implementation of budgetary constraints opened the door for the importing of market mechanisms into the public sector; council houses, for example, were sold off and replaced with, in a striking parallel with Reagan's urban-development approach, free-market enterprise zones. And like the Reagan administration, the Thatcher government maneuvered itself into direct conflict with organized labor, goading the miner's union into a year-long strike by closing many of the country's coal mines and offsetting the loss of supply with foreign exports. Just as the air-traffic controllers' strike in the United States would strike a fatal blow to the power of the country's labor movement as a whole, the ultimate failure of the miners' strike would mark a decline in the organizing capacity of the British working class.

Neoliberal Consolidation

The mode of neoliberalism launched by Reagan was not the only possible policy regime that the economic paradigm had to offer. Going back to its origins in the Walter Lippmann Colloquium, certain proto-neoliberal economists found themselves advocating not the unbridled *laissez-faire* system of the Austrian school, but a *social market economy* in which progressive state policies could co-exist alongside the activities of the free market. This approach was the hallmark of the Freiburg School of economics in Germany; known more commonly as ordoliberalism, it was their unique perspective that became the mode of development for the country's postwar reconstruction. Like the Austrians, the ordoliberals assumed that "the market, as a non-discriminating privilege-free order of competition, is in and by itself an ethical order."[22] Unlike the Austrians, however, the ordoliberals saw that this competition could still perpetuate social and economic inequality, and suggested the need for a "social insurance" that guaranteed a minimum of subsistence for those who were incapable, either temporarily or permanently, of selling their labor-power on the market. It should be noted that ordoliberalism differed fundamentally from Keynesianism and went to lengths to differentiate itself from it (though it would slip closer and closer to Keynesianism during the 1960s). Like its neoliberal cousins, ordoliberalism was principally concerned with supply-side as opposed to Keynesian demand-side, and rejected the strategy of building government deficits as a guide for monetary policy. Ordoliberalism and the social market economy, then, can be viewed as a sort of *third way* between Austrian (and later Chicago School) *laissez-faire* economics and Keynesian, social-democrat, and socialist alternatives.

Following the general crisis of Keynesianism in the 1970s and the overwhelming victory of the neoliberal-New Right opportunity structure in the 1980s, the Democratic Party found itself more or less without a compass, unable to maintain its relevancy in the face of the growing right-wing hegemony. In the mid-1980s, moderate Democrats began to rebuild the party in adherence with neoliberalism, adopting as they did the rhetoric of a "third way." In 1985 these politicians, who included senators

Bill Clinton and Al Gore, launched the Democratic Leadership Council (DLC), itself modeled directly on the New Right's successful coalition-building groups dating back to the early 70s. In their own words, the goal of the DLC was to "define and galvanize popular support for a new public philosophy built on progressive ideals, mainstream values, and innovative, non-bureaucratic, market-based solutions."[23] Wary of anything that might be considered "big government liberalism," the DLC advocated a reigning-in of high-budget spending, a reduction of deficits, and the creation of high-skill jobs, particularly in the information-communication technology sector. By the late 1980s, the DLC had forged a constructive alliance with the Progressive Policy Institute, a neoliberal pro-business think-tank that promoted "a philosophy that adapts the progressive tradition in American politics to the realities of the information age and points to a 'third way' beyond the liberal impulse to defend the bureaucratic status quo and the conservative bid to simply dismantle government." The DLC-Progressive Policy Institute nexus would become the hotbed for a new centrist political movement – the so-called "New Democrats."

Bill Clinton was the leading figure of the New Democrats, with the DLC and the Progressive Policy Institute serving as "idea mills" during his 1992 campaign, much in the manner that the Heritage Foundation had essentially drafted Reagan's legislative agenda. The two organizations also seized upon *Reinventing Government: How the Entrepreneurial Spirit is Transforming the Public Sector*, a book written by former journalist David Osborne and government consultant Ted Graebler that argued for a stripped-down government that approached politics with a business-oriented mentality. "Reinventing government" quickly became a slogan of choice for Clinton on the campaign trail, and Osborne himself was retained by the DLC to serve as a consultant. Following the election, Clinton directed Vice President Gore to launch the National Performance Review, a comprehensive review of the various federal agencies to find places where government bureaucracy could be curtailed for public-private partnerships and burdensome regulation could be replaced with market-friendly incentives. To assist with this work, Gore tapped Osborne to oversee some thirty different teams of federal workers. With the aid of Osborne (and funding from liberal-leaning philanthropies such as the Ford and Rockefeller Foundations), the National Performance Review would spawn the Alliance for Redesigning Government, which, like the DLC and the Progressive Policy Institute, aided in helping the Clinton administration shape its domestic and international policies. Again, this "re-designed government" was to come to resemble business more and more. In a policy paper endorsed by the Clinton administration, the Alliance suggested that:

> Government should be 1. A catalyst... 2. Community-owned... 3. Competitive... 4. Mission-driven... 5. Results oriented... 6. Customer-driven... 7. Enterprising... 8. Anticipatory... 9. Decentralized... 10. Market oriented.[24]

Unsurprisingly, given the uncompromising neoliberal outlook of the New Democrat's agenda, the Clinton administration's third way appears, in historical retrospect, as more or less the continuation of the Reaganite policy regime. For example, the North Atlantic Free Trade Agreement (NAFTA), signed into law by Clinton in 1994, had first been proposed by Reagan based on policies advocated by the Heritage Foundation.[25] NAFTA was billed as a platform for rapid job growth in the US states and Mexico alike, with Clinton asserting that liberalization of US trade with its southern neighbor would generate some 200,000 jobs. Likewise, NAFTA was intended to boost the Mexican economy through amplifying the structural adjustment programs that had already been applied by the IMF during the 1980s. This, however, would not be the case. A 2006 paper by the Economic Policy Institute records some 1,015,291 jobs lost in the US – predominantly in the manufacturing sector.[26] As a result, the great bulk of these displaced workers found themselves forced into the low-wage job sector, while many dropped out of the workforce altogether. Similarly, a study carried out in 2014 by the Center for Economic and Policy Research determined that NAFTA failed to "deliver the goods," so to speak, that it had promised to Mexico: inflation-adjusted wages have barely risen from the levels in 1980, while the unemployment rate doubled.[27] Additionally, in the time between the signing of NAFTA in 1994 and 2012, some 14.3 million people fell below the poverty line.

Clinton did indeed raise tax rates on the wealthy with the 1993 Deficit Reduction Act, a move that triggered virulent opposition from the Republicans and perhaps paved the way for the significant gains made by the party in the 1994 congressional election cycle. This conservative opposition to the New Democrat third way rallied behind the Contract for America, a text authored by Newt Gingrich that contained a series of policy recommendations drawn from the Heritage Foundation. Among these was a sweeping vision of welfare reform that placed limitations on those who could receive welfare, as well as work-requirement provisions intended to foster "individual responsibility." This would be the foundation of the Personal Responsibility and Work Opportunity Act, signed into law by Clinton in 1996. Described almost immediately by Peter Edelman (then the director of the Georgetown Center on Poverty, Inequality, and Public Policy) as "*the* major milestone in the political race to the bottom,"[28] the bill marked yet another major concession to the neoliberal consensus by placing a five-year limit on federal fund recipients, instituting a multi-year ban on welfare for legal immigrants, transitioning welfare into "workfare," and turning much of the control over welfare programs to the individual states.

The New Democrat interpretation of the third way thus

appears, in many respects, as not a repudiation of the neoliberal policy regime, but a consolidation of it. Both the Democrat and Republican parties came to hold nearly identical perspectives, albeit with minor differences (i.e. absolute *laissez-faire* versus a social market economy). These differences are so minor, in fact, that many Clinton-era policies can be viewed as the completion of what began in the Reagan era: liberalization of trade, the deconstruction of welfare (with both relying on overtly racist rhetoric),[29] deficit reduction and supply-side policies, and the weakening of organized labor. While the attack on labor had been carried out by Reagan's White House taking unprecedented aggression towards striking unions, it was Clinton's trade policies that continued this tendency. NAFTA was signed into law despite the opposition of the union movement, overriding objections by labor economists that the free-trade agreement would damage the working class. Clinton would also play a vital role in transforming the General Agreements on Tariffs and Trade (GATT, a multilateral trade agreement established by the United Nations in 1947) into the World Trade Organization (WTO). Alongside the IMF and the World Bank, the WTO is one of the primary hegemonic mechanisms for the globalization of neoliberalism, compelling nations to cut protectionist policies and open their borders to the flow of goods. Again, it is here that we can find Clinton completing the process that Reagan launched: the negotiations that led to the transformation of the GATT into the WTO were first launched by the Reagan administration in 1996.

When it came to financial capitalism, Clinton fully embraced the neoliberal perspective of the Chicago School. He retained Reagan and George Bush Sr.'s Federal Reserve chairman, Alan Greenspan, and for Secretary of Treasury he selected Robert Rubin – a Goldman Sachs executive who had spent time on the board of directors of the New York Stock Exchange. Rubin's protégé, Lawrence Summers, was brought on as the Deputy Secretary of the Treasury; previously, Summers had served on

Reagan's Council of Economic Advisers and spent several years as chief economist of the World Bank. Over the course of the administration, Rubin, Summers, and Greenspan would all work closely together and with the transnational neoliberal trade and development organizations. When the Asian Tigers (South Korea, Hong Kong, Taiwan, Singapore, Malaysia, Thailand, and Indonesia) were hit by a financial crisis in the late 90s, Rubin, Summers, and Greenspan worked hand-in-hand with the IMF to devise stabilization measures – earning them the title of "the committee to save the world" in a *Time* magazine article titled "The Three Marketeers."[30] Yet these stabilization measures were directly in line with the deregulatory, *laissez-faire* policies that had generated the crisis in the first place, and served to broaden the processes of neoliberalization that had been already been put in place by the WTO. For Greenspan, the crisis was "a very dramatic event towards a consensus of the type of market system which we have in in this country… [It] is likely to accelerate the dismantling in many Asian countries of the remnants of a system with large elements of government-directed investment."[31] Unsurprisingly, it was an American financial firm who stood to gain much from the "Three Marketeers'" actions. Wall Street, writes Naomi Klein,

"dispatched armies of bankers to the Asia-Pacific region to scout for brokerage firms, asset management firms, and even banks that they can snap up at bargain price. The hunt for Asian acquisition is urgent because many U.S. securities firms, led by Merrill Lynch and Co. and Morgan Stanley, have made overseas expansion their priority." In short order, several major sales went through: Merrill Lynch bought Japan's Yamaichi Securities as well as Thailand's largest securities firm, while AIG bought Bangkok Investment for a fraction of its worth. JP Morgan bought a stake in Kia Motors, while Travelers Group and Salomon Smith Barney bought one of Korea's largest textile companies as well as several other companies… Jeffrey

Garten, former U.S. undersecretary of commerce had predicted...
[that] there is going to be a significantly different Asia, and it will
be an Asia in which American firms have achieved much deeper
penetration, with greater access.[32]

The Contradiction of Hegemony

Even if the 1990s saw the consolidation of the neoliberal market
economy on a near global level, a contradiction mounted in the
growing tension between this rise of transnationally oriented
capital and the imperatives of national hegemony. Part and parcel
of this contradiction was the divergence of interests between
domestic political classes in various nations and the moneyed
interests that they represent. Across the 1990s, the United States
saw an influx of foreign capital in the form of investments, spear-
headed by Asian countries such as China and Japan. This, in turn,
triggered an outflow of American capital in the form of income
for these foreign investors. As the US transitioned from a creditor
nation to a debtor nation, which offset its deficits by borrowing
from foreign governments, the essential role of foreign capital in
maintaining US stability came to take on a political character. To
quote Arrighi:

...growing financial dependence on foreign governments necessarily
constrained US ability to pursue its national interest in the multi-
lateral and bilateral negotiations that promoted and regulated global
economic integration. In June 1997, for example, on his way back
from a G8 meeting in Denver that featured considerable chest-
thumping by the Clinton administration about the booming US
economy, the Japanese prime minister told a New York audience that
Japan had been tempted to sell large lots of US treasuries during
Japan's negotiations with the US over auto sales, and again when
exchange rates were fluctuating wildly while the United States
appeared preoccupied only with domestic issues. As one commen-

tator noted, Hashimoto "was simply reminding Washington that while it had created a robust... economy, Asian central banks held the deed".[33]

Nowhere would this contradiction be felt stronger than within the administration of George W. Bush. At a rather bewildering moment in American political history, we can see that Bush pursued a sort of "dual track" that sought to separate national affairs from international relations. In terms of domestic policy, the Bush administration pushed forward with the neoliberal program, as indicated not only by the "Bush tax cuts" of 2001 and 2003, but also the attacks on social security, the promotion of charter school programs, and the privatization of governmental agencies (such as FEMA, with disastrous effects during the devastation of New Orleans by Hurricane Katrina in 2005).[34] On the other hand, Bush's commitment to neoliberalism was tapered by a profound discomfort with the notion of globalization; to quote one White House aide in 2003, Bush "thinks what went wrong in the 90's is that we forgot to put American interests first. So globalization sounds like the creation of a lot of rules that may restrict the president's choices, that dilute American influence."[35] By extension, the international-relations agenda pursued by Bush eschewed the neoliberal rhetoric of globalization and embraced instead neoconservativism, marking a return to the sort of balance between free-market approaches and strong national unilateralism, particularly in regards to defense issues.

The roots of the neoconservatism of the Bush era were laid in the 1990s, and can only be contextualized by the perceived loss of power on behalf of the United States in the international arena. In 1997, several elements of the old neoliberal-New Right opportunity structure – the American Enterprise Foundation, and the Scaife and Bradley Foundations – launched the Project for the New American Century (PNAC). With many members drawn from the ranks of the Cold Warriors, the PNAC's goal was to lobby the Clinton administration to adopt a more hawkish approach to international relations by taking a strong stance against dictatorships in the Middle East and elsewhere, and by increasing the annual defense budget to build-up an American military superiority. When Bush came to power, a large number of PNAC members took central positions in his administration – including Vice President Dick Cheney, Secretary of Defense Donald Rumsfeld, Undersecretary of Defense (and World Bank president) Paul Wolfowitz, and several members of the National Security Council. After the events of September 11th, this structure was able to cynically seize the opportunity provided by the crisis in a bid to usher in, to quote one of the PNAC's policy documents, a "*Pax Americana*" founded upon "unquestioned U.S. military preeminence."[36]

The PNAC playbook, which the Bush administration sought to follow, called for preemptive strikes against dictatorships not only in Iraq, but also in Iran, Syria, and other surrounding countries, and their replacement with US-friendly client regimes. At the same time, this was not simply an affair of a country flexing its muscles against antagonistic states. In 2001, Vice President Cheney commissioned a report on "energy security" to be carried out by the Council on Foreign Relations; the findings suggested that Western economic and political interests required a steady flow of oil from the vast Iraqi oil reserves – and that the policies pursued by the Hussein government stood to project volatility into the world market.[37] By removing Hussein and restructuring the Iraqi oil industry, the United States would stand to reap enormous benefits beyond simple geopolitical posturing. As David Harvey puts it, "whoever controls the Middle East controls the global oil spigot, and whoever controls the global oil spigot can control the global economy, at least for the near future."[38] A successful venture in Iraq, then, would solve the contradiction between the global market economy and American unilateral hegemony.

Reality, of course, has not been so straightforward. The intervention against Hussein entailed an ambitious project of nation building, which the Bush administration pursued through the forceful privatization of Iraq's nationalized industries and the introduction of market mechanisms into society at the hands of the Coalition Provisional Authority (CPA). This move, described by *The Economist* as a "wish-list that foreign investors and donor agencies dream of for developing markets,"[39] made any future success of the national economy rely on the foreign capital of rich countries. Yet with borders open, imports and foreign workers poured into the country, driving out of business innumerable beleaguered Iraqi firms. With all restrictions removed, money moved out of the country – a scenario that was compounded by the CPA's "de-Baathification program," which saw the firing of some 500,000 state workers. Without a functioning economy or a solid government, and under the martial law imposed by the CPA, an insurgency mounted that would drag the United States into a deeper and more protracted conflict than it had anticipated.

The violent misstep in Iraq by the Bush administration was matched by mounting discontent at home. As the war grew longer and uglier, the fervent patriotism that had surged forward following September 11th waned. The war itself became a scandal, as news reports revealed the depth of cronyism and war profiteering at play in Iraq: from Cheney's relationship with Halliburton, to the Bush family's own with the Carlyle Group, to the uncountable number of advisers connected to defense firms, it became clear that those who had advocated for the war – and those who were managing it – stood to personally profit from it. Revelations about programs such as the Total Information Awareness project, which promised not only to usher in a surveillance state beyond the PATRIOT Act, but to create a financial system where people could bet and speculate on the likelihood of terrorist attacks, showed how far outside the realm of "normal conduct" the administration had gone.[40] And finally, controversies arose over the entire nature of the invasion of Iraq – what exactly, people asked, did Iraq and Hussein have to do with al-Qaeda and Afghanistan? In this context, an anti-war movement arose to contest the Bush administration's new – and ultimately doomed – neoconservative synthesis.

The effects of Bush's domestic policies also aided in turning the tide against the president. When Hurricane Katrina ravaged New Orleans, the underfunded and privatized civil services found themselves outmatched by the humanitarian catastrophe. The role of things like the Bush tax cuts were pointed to as the source for the depreciation of national emergency-response mechanisms as well as the crumbling infrastructures; after having been obscured by the boom-time of the Clinton years, the rift between the wealthy financial and political classes and the poor was highlighted. It also spoke volumes to the fact that the hardest-hit communities were not only poor, but minorities. Bush's plummeting poll numbers were a measure of dissatisfaction not only with the president, but at a more generalized and diffused state of affairs: the fundamental disconnect between the levers of government and the increasingly marginalized sectors of the citizenry. Likewise, Bush found himself facing mounting pressure from a renewed labor movement, having pursued greater anti-union measures than any president since Reagan (including the appointing of anti-labor advocates to the US Department of Labor and the National Labor Relations Board, banning strikes, ordering striking workers to return to work, and the utilization of executive order to roll back union rights for federal employees).[41]

Attempted Resolution

The presidential campaign of Senator Barack Obama appeared as a national reset of the sort of policies and overall political attitudes embodied by the Bush administration. Under the rhetoric of "Hope and Change", the era of blatant cronyism, and the atmosphere of paranoia that it engendered, appeared to be over. As the Great Recession loomed and the war dragged into another year, the Democratic Party stood to gain considerably from the eight years of repeated failures on the behalf of the Republican Party to appear even modestly beholden to the general constituency. Forming itself as the progressive solution to neoconservativism, the Obama campaign was a paradigm-shifting social-media blitz – drawing on, in large part, the momentum of the anti-war movement.

A major link between the grassroots anti-war movement and Obama can be found in a large umbrella organization called Americans Against Escalation in Iraq (AAEI), which lasted from 2006 to 2008. With funding provided by labor unions such as the SEIU and Democrat-aligned think-tanks like the Center for American Progress, as well as organizing carried out by Democrat-linked organizations such as MoveOn, the AAEI sought to initially put pressure on Congress to end the war. By 2007, however, this agenda was dropped, and the AAEI shifted gears to a milder demand: that President Bush refrain from entering into agreements with the new Iraqi government that would establish long-term troop deployment in the country. Shortly thereafter, the AAEI's chief campaign manager, MoveOn's Tom Matzzie, established a spin-off organization called the Campaign for America's Future. This new organization concentrated the bulk of its energies on grassroots lobbying against Republican candidates, anti-Republican and pro-Democrat television ad campaigns, and raising money and awareness for the Obama campaign – which tied directly to the senator's supposed opposition to war.

The slogan of "Hope and Change," however, not only spoke to the need for an exit from the war, but also embodied a spirit of economic populism that appealed to marginalized minorities and disenfranchised workers. Obama enjoyed large support from the large labor unions: the SEIU, the UCFW, and AFL-CIO all endorsed the candidate and donated large sums of money and organizers to the campaign. Much was made of Obama's time spent as an organizer in Chicago's low-income communities, having worked with the Developing Communities Project, the Gamaliel Foundation, the Woods Fund, and the Joyce Foundation. This long interaction with community development and social-justice activism returned again and again over the course of Obama's campaign, particularly in his calls for a new "bottom-up economics" and his attacks on free-trade deals like NAFTA that boasted "plenty of protections for corporations and their profits, but none for our environment or our workers."[42] Yet perhaps the staunchest depiction of Obama's claim to economic populism is to be found in his autobiography *The Audacity of Hope*, in which he describes the United States as:

> *a nation even more stratified economically and socially... one in which an increasingly prosperous knowledge class, living in exclusive enclaves, will be able to purchase whatever they want on the marketplace—private schools, private health care, private security, and private jets—while a growing number of their fellow citizens are consigned to low-paying service jobs, vulnerable to dislocation, pressed to work longer hours, depending on an under-funded, overburdened, and underperforming public sector for their health care, retirement, and their children's educations.*[43]

Writing this in the twilight of the Obama administration, it is clear to see that this picture has not changed, and in many instances, this reality has only been exacerbated. Likewise, the neoconservative war project rumbles onward, albeit with a slightly altered face that resembles less the reckless unilateralism of the Bush administration than the humanitarian interven-tionism of the Clinton administration. And while Obama might have criticized free-trade deals that undercut the livelihoods of the working class, he currently presides over the Trans-Pacific Partnership agreement, a trade deal that will all but lock into place the neoliberal hegemony over the entirety of the Pacific region of production and trade. How does one situate these realities, as well as the host of perplexing turns in the Obama administration, with this depiction of Obama as a progressive leader?

To begin unraveling Obama's relationship to the neoliberal ideology, we can look to the environment where Obama spent a considerable amount of time as a lecturer on constitutional law: the University of Chicago. It was here, by his own admission, that he encountered the market orthodoxy of Milton Friedman, which he readily consumed in an attempt to produce a synthesis with more socially-conscious social-democratic attitudes. Such a synthesis appears unlikely, even if such a thing had been attempted earlier by the Clintonite Third Way; either way, it is arguable that it was the neoliberal side that won out over social democracy. Cass Sunstein, a close friend of Obama at the university (and the president's "regulation czar"), described him as "a University of Chicago Democrat, so he's very attuned to the virtue of free markets and the risks of free-market regulation. He's not an old-style Democrat who's excited about regulations [for their own sake]."[44] Reflecting on these influences, Obama himself would later state during an interview with CNBC "Look, I'm a pro-growth, free-market guy; I love the market."

Obamanomics, as it came to be called, would come together in the Brookings Institute's Hamilton Project, launched in 2006 by Robert Rubin with funding provided by Goldman Sachs. The stated goal of the Hamilton Project was a striking resurrection of the neoliberal concept of the state – that is, a return to analyzing the way that fiscal, monetary, and social policy could effectively enhance the functioning of the free market without intervening directly within it. While maintaining an ostensibly centrist perspective, the Hamilton Project certainly leans towards neoliberalism, particularly in regards to its outlook towards financial capitalism. This is due to the role of Rubin in organizing the project, and the funding of Goldman Sachs (where, as we may recall, Rubin spent twenty-six years, including several as co-chairman). There is thus a direct continuity between President Clinton's pro-Wall Street policy team and the Hamilton Project; indeed, besides Rubin, the Project's director Peter Orszag had served as senior economist and senior adviser to Clinton's Council of Economic Advisers. Obama himself would speak at the Hamilton Project's initial launch, lauding their "pragmatist" perspective and commitment to fostering economic opportunity (as opposed to a class-based interpretation of economics). When he assembled his own economic advisory team on the campaign trail he drew heavily from the Project's ranks, tapping not only Orszag, but Lawrence Summers (Clinton's former Treasury Secretary and former Rubin acolyte), Austan Goolsbee, and Jason Furman (a staunch defender of Wal-Mart's business model, which earned the Obama campaign criticism from the labor movement). These individuals were joined by Timothy Geithner (a Rubin protégé from the Clinton Treasury and a key negotiator in the Bush bail-outs) and Paul Volcker (Reagan's architect of the interest-rate shocks). This coterie of individuals would earn Obama the title of a "Wall Street Democrat," and flavored the economic approach of the Obama administration as a whole. Summers would become the director of the National Economic Council, with Furman serving as one of his deputies (and later becoming chairman of the president's Council of Economic Advisers); Geithner would be appointed as Secretary of the Treasury. Goolsbee would do a stint as chairman of the Council of Economic Advisers, while Orszag would be selected to head up the Office of Budget and Management.

Thus the incoming Obama administration found itself suspended between two contradictory positions – one of economic populism motivated by grass-roots leftist demands, and the other a business-as-usual neoliberalism seeking damage control in the wake of the Bush administration and the onset of the Great Recession. It was clear, given the entrenched power of the Democratic Party establishment and its relationship to the interests of finance capital, which side would gain superiority over the other. An earlier indication of this was Obama's approach to NAFTA. On the campaign trail, the soon-to-be president vowed to renegotiate the deal and bring international civil-society organizations into trade summit meetings – but within a year the pledge was shelved. By 2010 all commitments to fix flaws in existing trade deals (particularly in regards to labor standards and environmental protections) seemed to have disappeared, replaced by an apparent onslaught of new free-trade deals and trade talks. The free-trade deal with South Korea in 2010, for example, was lauded as an engine for domestic job growth through increased exports. Over the course of the following three years, however, exports from the United States to South Korea steadily declined, while imports from South Korea rose.[45]

When it came to crisis management during the Great Recession, Obamanomics took on a more schizophrenic character that nonetheless reflected the interests of financial capital. The bail-out of the auto industry, carried out under the gaze of Summers and Geithner and implemented by Wall Street investment banker and financier Steven Rattner, followed the path of strong government intervention to the point of quasi-nationalization. Some $82 million was pumped into the auto-manufacturing sector, while Rattner's team fired General Motor's chairman Rick Wagoner and steered both GM and Chrysler into controlled bankruptcy. The assets of each were then sold to allow the respective companies to emerge anew; at the end of the aggressive series of moves, GM was owned by the United States Treasury (which would begin selling off its shares of the company, a process that was completed in 2013) and Chrysler was owned by Fiat and the United Auto Workers (UAW) labor union. While these structures stood with much to gain from the re-organization, the conditions for the labor force were arguably worse off: in exchange for government funding and intervention, the UAW agreed to allow Ford, Chrysler, and GM to pay new hires significantly lower wages, provide shorter time off, and receive not pension plans but "personal retirement funds."

In the financial sector, however, government intervention went on to take a radically different form. Bush's TARP program, ushered in by the Emergency Economic Stabilization Act of 2008, was Obama's engine of choice (this was unsurprising, given Obama's support as a senator for Bush's measures). What this meant was that while workers in the industrial sector had to face cut-backs under a hands-on approach, the financial sector was treated at arm's length, with the bankers and traders facing none of the repercussions that the leadership of GM endured. As Joseph Stiglitz wrote, "Low-income workers who had worked all their life and done nothing wrong would have to take a wage cut, but not the million-dollar plus financiers who had brought the world to the brink of financial ruin."[46] When Obama confronted the interests of a finance capital in a 2009 speech, he opted to reiterate his commitment to the neoliberal economic paradigm: "make no mistake, this administration is committed to pursuing expanded trade and new trade agreements [which are] absolutely essential to our economic future."[47] Regulations were proposed to reign in the excesses of finance capitalism, but again, when addressing the financiers he chose not to take a hard stance against their actions. Abandoning all pretense of the populist rhetoric that the electorate had witnessed on the campaign trail, the president beseeched the finance class to work with the government and mind their "obligations and responsibility" to the nation. Here, too, the neoliberal ideology finds its stark reflection: instead of ensuring "responsible economic activity," any possible regulation on market activity would not be deployed in a way that restrained this activity; instead, it would help to prod and guide the market towards its most "efficient" state.

These same priorities could be found at play in Obama's stimulus policies. While certain left-leaning economists (including a handful inside of Obama's own economic team) rallied for a large-scale stimulus package modeled on the New Deal, Obama was reluctant to move towards any economic formulas that moved against the consensus. The stimulus package that emerged, instead, would total $787 billion – nearly 40% of which went to tax cuts.[48] A large portion of the remainder went not to federally-funded jobs programs, but to state- and local-level governments for immediate fiscal relief. By 2010, new measures were deployed to try and pivot the economy towards recovery. As Keynesian economists clamored for fiscal policy that would boost consumer purchasing power, Obama's Federal Reserve, led by Ben Bernanke, embraced instead quantitative easing (QE) as its strategy of choice. Through QE, capital could flow directly into the banks, who would then provide loans (incentivized by low interest rates) and by extension allow money to circulate in the economy. The power of finance capital is built into the structure of QE: it is the banks who find themselves the benefactors of government assistance, which allows them in turn to profit from debtors as the economy (presumably) turns and grows with a correlating interest-rate increase. In the case of the United States – as well as in Europe, where similar policies were pursued – QE money often went straight into corporate profits, into the Federal Reserve and other central banks, and back into the finance markets as opposed to entering the real economy. In both the United States and the United Kingdom, a distinctive correlation between QE policies and rising income inequality developed.[49] Nonetheless, it is clear that the mechanisms deployed to fight the recession were wholly in line with the neoliberal orthodoxy.

Breakdown

The Tea Party

Arriving on the scene in 2009, the Tea Party movement was the most vocal opponent of the Obama administration, charging that the presidency was ushering in an era of "big-government" liberalism that would infringe on the rights of the everyday people and, by extension, constrain the ability of small businesses to grow through burdensome regulation and red tape. Egged on by right-wing media pundits, the Obama administration was increasingly identified as a "socialist" government. Evidence for this, the conservative populists suggested, could be found in Obama's time spent as a community organizer, his attempts to appoint "reformed" socialists such as Van Jones to his administration, and his endorsement by organizations such as the Communist Party USA and the Democratic Socialists of America (organizations that, historically, have consistently endorsed Democrats against Republicans). The Tea Party rallied itself against this perceived left-wing conspiracy by hoisting up a campaign promoting lower tax rates (endorsing a flat tax as opposed to progressive tax), deregulation (particularly where environmental protections were concerned), and a transfer of governmental power from the federal to state level.

In reality, the conflict engendered by the Tea Party was not so much a case of the citizenry against the government, or a referendum on the nation's future as a whole, but a signal of the breakdown of the neoliberal consensus. It was, put most simply, a conflict between diverging opinions on the nature of the neoliberal project: on one hand, the continuation of post-Third Way neoliberalism, as promoted by Obama and the finance class, and on the other hand, a turn to the sort of "small-government" neoliberalism initially advocated by the members of the Mont

Pelerin Society. This conflict was inscribed in the nature of the Tea Party from the moment of its inception, arising from the failure of libertarian Ron Paul's 2008 presidential campaign. While never the choice of the Republican establishment (and, in fact, quite ostracized from it, perhaps due to his courting of the anti-war movement by taking an adversarial stance on the conflicts in Iraq and Afghanistan), Paul's philosophical outlook derives almost wholly from the Austrian proto-neoliberals F.A. Hayek and Ludwig von Mises – marking a break with even the Friedmanite interpretations of neoliberalism. As detailed in his book *End the Fed*, Paul's vision is one of a market economy detached from undue influence of social regulation; policies like those that would be advanced by the Obama administration to deal with the Great Recession – quantitative easing, the lowering of exchange rates, and the creation of money, for example – would distort the market by altering its natural state. Knocked from this abstracted ideal, the market would be unable to recover, finding itself detached from the realities of supply and demand.

While the Tea Party emerged from Paul's support base, as it gained momentum the specific Austrian peculiarities of his campaign faded into a more generalized classical neoliberal perspective. While continuing with the "libertarian" label that Paul had popularized, its core demands focused on deregulation, anti-labor policies, and pro-corporate mandates combined with appeals to patriotism and, quite frequently, Christian morals and values. Despite appearing as a legitimate grassroots movement, the Tea Party from its institutional inception was a carefully crafted spectacle managed and directed by the very members of the capitalist class these policies would assist. Its growth was fueled by none other than the old neoliberal-New Right opportunity structure: early protests, such as the Tax Day Protest that marked the launch of the Tea Party proper, were organized primarily by two organizations – FreedomWorks and Americans for Prosperity. The origins of FreedomWorks lay in the Citizens for a Sound Economy (CSE), a pro-market think-tank founded in the 1980s by the Koch brothers to act as a "sales force that participated in political campaigns, or town hall meetings, in rallies, to communicate to the public at large much of the information that these think tanks [i.e. the neoliberal think-tanks summarized earlier in this chapter] were creating."[50] In 2004, the CSE merged with Empower America, an organization affiliated with the Claremont Institute – yet another neoliberal think-tank funded by right-wing philanthropies, including the Scaife, Bradley, and Olin foundations. This merger resulted in the creation of FreedomWorks, which would also receive extremely large funding from the Scaife, Bradley, and Olin foundations, as well as money from the Koch Foundation and Koch Industries.

Americans for Prosperity (AFP), too, can be traced back to these same organizations, having been launched in 2003 by members of the CSE just prior to its merger with Empower America. Just like with FreedomWorks, the AFP's activities are financed by this same donor network, with the usual right-wing philanthropies making large grants to the organization. The bulk of this money comes from the Koch brothers, usually passed through intermediary organizations such as the pro-market nonprofit Freedom Partners, the anti-Obamacare Center to Protect Patient's Rights, and the Independent Women's Forum, an anti-feminist and climate-change denial organization – all of which are subsidized by Koch money. To close the ties further, David Koch sits on the AFP's board of directors, while the organization's director, Nancy Pfotenhauer, was the former head of Koch Industries' Washington office. Besides organizing protests, marches, and rallies, the AFP in 2009 launched bus tours across the nation to rally supporters against Obamacare, climate-change legislation, and tax and regulatory policies, giving rise to a separate organization called Tea Party Express. In a similar vein, FreedomWorks launched a subsidiary organization called the Tea Party Patriots, which effectively obscured the Koch roots of the movement while organizing protests across the country.

This rejection of the Obama administration was matched by an increasingly obstructionist Republican Party inside the halls of government that sought to block or at least slow down the majority of the president's moves, from healthcare reform to district and circuit appointees. The Tea Party movement would escalate this tendency. During the 2010 mid-term elections, candidates operating under the Tea Party banner totaled 129 running for the House and 9 for the Senate; 5 of these candidates would enter the Senate, while 40 entered into the House. In 2010 the congressional Tea Party Caucus was launched, which despite its smaller numbers was able to gain an exorbitant amount of influence in Congress (through determining the outcome of swing votes and brokering compromises between various Republican factions), pulling the trajectory of the party further to the right. This congressional caucus found its counterpart in the Senate with the launch of an informal Tea Party Caucus, organized in part by Ron Paul's son, Rand Paul. Both of these formal and informal caucuses worked closely with the organizations that backed the Tea Party protests, including Americans for Prosperity, FreedomWorks, the Tea Party Express, as well as Americans for Tax Reform and the National Taxpayers Union.

As stressed earlier, Obama's policies throughout these periods preferred to enable, not hinder, market mechanisms in regard to both trade and finance policy as well as broad social policies. In the case of climate-change legislation, for instance, the solution was the market-friendly cap-and-trade policies, which would effectively create a private market for carbon credits. When it came to healthcare reform, the solution proposed was not a system of socialized medicine, but a mandate system that benefited private insurance companies. Insofar as labor policies were concerned, we can see in the approach to the auto industry bail-out a desire to retain the power of organized labor, albeit in a more restrained and "reasonable" form. For the Tea Party on both the grassroots and governmental levels, these moderate policies were beyond the pale of any acceptable legislation in the neoliberal world. The members of the Tea Party inside both the Congress and Senate, alongside their private benefactors, mounted a vigorous attack on these policies, gaining further concessions on the healthcare bill and eliminating the possibility of any constructive debate on climate change.

The Tea Party movement's sharpest attack was on organized labor in Wisconsin in early 2011, carried out by Governor Scott Walker, who had entered into office after riding the Tea Party election wave of 2010. To battle a budget deficit he proposed a piece of legislation entitled the Wisconsin Budget Repair Bill, containing a lengthy series of provisions that cut pensions for state workers, sold state-owned energy companies, and stripped many union workers of collective bargaining rights, while limiting the bargaining rights of other workers to capped wages with shortened contracts. When the state's Democrat senators left the state to avoid the passage of the bill, Wisconsin Republicans ordered their arrest – a ploy that failed when law-enforcement officers could not cross state lines. Only after a series of other tactics (including depriving senators of their pay, banning Democratic staffers from using copy machines, and threatening to begin laying off state employees) that failed, Walker slightly adjusted the bill; when they continued to refuse to vote on the measure, the Republicans exploited a loophole and passed the bill on March 11th. As a result, there was a precipitous decline of state aid to schools, large worker lay-offs, and a declining public union membership rate.

The battle over the Budget Repair Bill became a flashpoint for civil unrest. On February 14th, the day after Walker proposed the bill, tens of thousands of protestors flooded the area around the state's capitol building, increasing up to some 30,000 the following day. By the 17th, protests spread to other states such as Ohio, where Tea Party-aligned Governor John Kasich was considering similar anti-union measures. The protests reached their height on February 26th, as between 70,000 and 100,000 protestors and activists flooded into Wisconsin's capital, many of them union-affiliated workers brought in from out of state by the AFL-CIO and the Teamsters. Simultaneously, counter-protests grew, their numbers drawing from the Tea Party grassroots. The majority of these Tea Party counter-protests were organized by American Majority, a non-profit aimed at recruiting and training Tea Party activists to run in local elections. American Majority's funding came primarily from an organization called the Sam Adams Alliance; the Alliance's principle organizer and manager, in term, was revealed to have been affiliated with both the Citizens for a Sound Economy and Americans for Prosperity. This did not go unnoticed by the pro-union protestors, and when it became known that David Koch had been a major donor in Walker's initial campaign for governor, the protests grew again, moving their target from the Capitol to the Wisconsin Manufacturers and Commerce, the state's primary business lobbying group. As a response, the Tea Party rallies too grew in size, bringing Republic media icons such as Andrew Breitbart and Sarah Palin to the state to give speeches.

It must be stressed again, as we did earlier, that the Tea Party marked an instability in the neoliberal regime, albeit a sort of muddled and confusing one. On one hand, the libertarian origins pointed at once to what was considered to be simultaneously a purely free-trade economic platform and an alleged return to America's constitutional basis; on the other hand, the bulk of the movement was steered by forces that wanted to push back against the sort of centrist neoliberalism presented by the likes of Clinton and Obama. These two contingencies were joined by a more nationalistic support base that was less interested in free trade – or economic neoliberalism, for that matter. The goal of this base, culled at large from a white and Christian middle class, was to see a return to American strength and prosperity. This has been indicated, for example, by the consistent repudiations of proposals for amnesty for immigrants (a topic we will return to shortly). The Tea Party, in other words, was a kind of mirror-image of the neoliberal-New Right opportunity structure that flourished in the 1970s: the collision of and coordination between libertarian economics, social conservatism, and nationalism. Just as the previous opportunity structure arose to grasp the crisis of the 1970s, the current one builds itself in the ongoing crisis of the Great Recession.

Occupy Wall Street

In mid-2011, a very different sort of grassroots movement emerged in the United States. Unlike the Tea Party, this movement was militantly left-wing, refused to engage in the electoral process, and did not aim to defend the free market against a mythical encroachment of the government on its actions. Instead, its target was finance capitalism itself, pointing an accusing finger at the central role of finance in the 2008 crisis, the elite-serving nature of the bail-outs and recovery program, and the overall tendency towards wealth inequality that had accumulated at both the national and international levels across the neoliberal era. This movement was Occupy Wall Street (OWS), kicking off on September 17th, 2011, when some 2,000 protestors congregated in Zuccotti Park, a "privately owned public space" in the heart of New York City's financial district. As the protestors claimed the park as theirs and set up a self-governed encampment, their numbers swelled to gigantic proportions. Through mainstream and social media, the movement was able to spread: "By mid-October demonstrations were underway or planned for 951 cities in 82 countries."[51]

The issue of income inequality led the Occupy movement to adopt an incredibly class-oriented nature, highlighted by its analysis of the "99% and the 1%" – the 1% being the wealthiest Americans who held the majority of wealth accumulated in the

United States, and the 99% being the broad and open-ended "everybody else" who saw their wages, incomes, and general livelihood declining. At the same time, the internal structuring of Occupy deviated radically from traditional class-based coalitions and workers' movements. Eschewing electoral politics was part of this approach, which drew heavily on "post-political politics" such as anarchism, post-anarchism, Situationism, autonomous Marxism, and network-based movements such as the Zapatistas as sign-posts for how to organize. Hierarchy was to be warded off at all costs, leading the movement to adopt a horizontalist model of direct democracy that utilized open general assemblies – and later, with much failure, spokes councils – as a tool for informal governance. These general assemblies, in turn, relied on a process of "modified consensus" that was intended to allow every participant a say in decisions – while also hoping to prevent majorities from dominating the consensus in spite of minorities.

This model led to some tensions between Occupy and contingencies from organized labor led by the AFL-CIO and the SEIU. Despite a Labor Outreach Committee organized at the start of OWS, workers were often constrained by structural limitations imposed on them by the larger labor federations – a seeming confirmation of Occupy's hesitancy towards hierarchy and centralization.[52] In another notable instance, SEIU organizers assisting OWS in New York City attempted to use the platform to campaign for President Obama. This is not so say that the alliance between Occupy and labor was not fruitful; in early December, for example, Occupy Oakland and the International Longshore and Warehouse Union (ILWU) were able to shut down a significant number of ports across the West Coast (this action did, however, bring the ILWU into conflict with the AFL-CIO, who opposed the action). For the occupiers – and for many workers who endorsed militant actions even if their leadership shirked away from it – these conflicts and the inability of the union leadership to throw their weight behind a large, class-based movement revealed the latent conservatism of government and business-aligned organized labor.

The arrival of the movement in September, and its rapid escalation across the country and beyond, caught off-guard not only the organized labor federations but the government as a whole. Its sudden appearance was puzzling – why would such a force appear, in mid-2011, when the damage done by the financial crisis and the blatant cronyism of the bail-out had already passed? There are multiple catalyzing factors that fueled the growth of OWS. The first of these was the figure of Obama himself. As a study carried out by the New York City-based Murphy Institute showed, 90% of OWS members polled voted in the 2008 election cycle, 89% of which voted for Obama.[53] Of this 89%, some 40% actively took part in the 2008 election campaign. As the Murphy Institute's on-the-ground research illustrated, the majority of these individuals supported Obama and even worked for the campaign due to the appeal of his left-of-center rhetoric and history as a community organizer. David Graeber, one of the early organizers of Occupy at Zuccotti Park, pointed out that for many of these people, Obama "was one of the few candidates in recent memory who could be said to have emerged from a social movement background rather than from smoke-filled rooms. This, combined with the fact that Obama was Black, gave young people a sense that they were experiencing a genuinely transformative moment."[54] The decline of Obama's image as a grassroots progressive and the rise of the reality of Obama as a neoliberal Democrat caused many supporters of the president to, in the words of an Organizer for Obama-turned-Occupier, say "'Let's try something completely different.'"

Another crucial step towards Occupy was the outburst of protests that followed the anti-labor bill advanced in Wisconsin under Tea Party Republican governor Scott Walker (as discussed earlier). There was a direct continuity between the styles of protest and organizing of the "kill-the-bill" movement and OWS, with the events in Wisconsin acting as a sort of "Occupy before Occupy." Just as the Occupiers seized Zuccotti Park and held it until police-backed repression in November of 2011, the Wisconsin protestors maintained a constant presence at the state's central capitol building – an occupation that was dubbed "The People's House." Incensed by the actions in Wisconsin, protestors in New York City recreated the People's House on March 30th, holding a short-lived occupation of the capitol building in reaction to Governor Andrew Cuomo's planned austerity bill. It was here that the seeds of OWS were sown – and where the rhetoric of the 99% and the 1% first emerged.[55] When OWS was formally launched in September, activists from both the People's House in Wisconsin and the anti-austerity protests played a vital role in organizing and maintaining the long-term occupation.

In the line running from the Wisconsin protests in NYC during March to Occupy's quick ascendency, we can note three interconnected – and ultimately directly related – elements at play in "civil society" during 2011. The first of these was a massive rejection of neoliberalism, which took differing priorities in different phases. The Wisconsin protests emerged in a localized context, but caught fire due to their ability to hone in the fact that neoliberalism was dissolving the power of labor; in the course of the protests, it became clear that the attack on labor and the imposition of austerity by the government were bound together in a single agenda – that is, the neoliberal policy regime. By the time the cycle of struggles built into Occupy, the recognition of neoliberalism's profoundly anti-democratic mechanics came to include income inequality at large, encompassing the repression of minorities, the ongoing struggle for gender rights, the corrosive power of finance capital, and the rising tide of debt (with a particular focus on homeowner debt and student debt). This, in turn, signals the second element: a categorical rejection, by those on the left, of the neoliberal faction rising from the Tea

Party. This can be glimpsed by the nature of the Wisconsin protests, which emerged as a rejection of a Tea Party politician and would see the direct confrontation of left-leaning protestors with Tea Party conservatives. By the time Occupy reached its height, the role of rich right-wing donors such as the Koch Brothers in subsidizing the Tea Party at the grassroots and their counterparts in the political arena had become common knowledge; rejection of this tendency of "election-buying" would too become assimilated into the movement's main concerns.

This brings us, finally, to the third element: the rejection of traditional bourgeois democracy and all its trappings, and by extension, the experience of everyday life in a bourgeois-dominated society. Starting in Wisconsin, a fundamentally new (to the US, at least) approach to politics was happened upon, one in which the boundary between everyday life and politics was erased, in turning causing life to be experienced in a new, dynamic way. In Occupy, the nature of this transformation became apparent and what on the surface was ostensibly a protest against finance capital maintained, below the surface, a desperate plea for the means to realize new ways to experience life in terms of experimenting with the spaces of lived experience. Hence the rationale behind Occupy's famous rejection of demands: the demands were always present, implicit in the organization of the movement itself.

Occupy, however, was not the first movement in 2011 that sought to challenge the dominant structures of power by seizing public space. The movement, in fact, appeared very late when compared to the Arab Spring revolts that tore across the Middle East – itself a postcolonial insurgency against the remnants of the West's imperialism.[56] Likewise, "take-the-squares" movements had sprung up across Europe, primarily in countries that were hit the hardest by neoliberal austerity programs: Greece, Spain, Portugal, Ireland, so on and so forth. Under names such as the *Indignados*, the demands of the earlier alter-globalization movement[57] were pushed into the new, post-recession, post-War on Terror world. Given the global nature of this cycle of revolts – and the similar, if not identical, ways in which dissenting civil-society actors expressed democracy – we can say that 2011 was the year in which people came to reject the neoliberal mode of capitalism and its designs for their everyday lives. While the Middle East would see the toppling of dictators (and in some cases, the installation of new ones) and left-wing parties such as Podemos in Spain and Syriza in Greece would rise from the 2011 revolts, it would take nearly half a decade for politicians in the US to listen to the demands of civil society. But first, we turn now to the political ramifications of the Tea Party movement.

Breakdown (2): The 2016 Election Cycle

The 2016 election was intended to be the election that fulfilled the ambitions of the Tea Party movement. The majority of the Republican candidate pool was drawn from the ranks of those affiliated with the Tea Party: presidential hopefuls Ted Cruz, Marco Rubio, and Rand Paul were amongst those swept into office by the Tea Party wave, along with John Kasich, a long-time political player who re-entered public office with Tea Party support in 2010. Furthermore, each of these individuals relied on money from right-wing donors such as the Koch Brothers during both their initial election campaigns and their presidential campaigns.[58] Rubio received money directly from Koch Industries consistently between the years of 2010 and 2016, and in 2012 and 2014 received money from the Club for Growth, an integral part of the Koch donor network. Cruz, meanwhile, enjoyed Koch Industries funding in 2012, while in the 2014 election cycle and 2016 presidential campaign he received large sums from the Club for Growth and the Senate Conservative Fund – yet another node in the right's dark-money complex. Rand Paul was the recipient of Koch Industries money in 2010,

2012, 2014, and 2016, Club for Growth money in 2012 and 2014, and money from Citizens United – a conservative donor clearing-house – in 2014 and 2016. John Kasich, meanwhile, received Koch Industries money in 2012 and 2014, with funding dropping off in the 2016 election cycle. Notably, Kasich was deeply involved in the formative years of the American Legislative Exchange Council – founded in the 1970s by members of the neoliberal-New Right opportunity structure and today a recipient of funding from the Koch Brothers and other right-wing billion-aires.

What we have, then, is a long-term movement and political strategy seeking first, as we saw earlier, to realign the parameters of political and economic conservatism from the bottom-up (even if that bottom-up is, in actuality, top-down), and then to use the momentum generated from the realignment to steer the system away from the Democrats' Third Way-esque interpretation of neoliberalism – embodied by the alleged "reformism" of the Obama administration. If one was to abstract away the complex network of donor organizers and the conservative millionaires and billionaires who move their money through them, the picture that would emerge (that is, the image that is intended to be seen) is one in which a democratically-conscious movement swelled up from the population and set the country on its "proper track" – a proper track that coincidently consisted of the largest set of pro-business policies imaginable, from the repealing of taxation to the removal of environmental regulations to the privatization of social services.

This picture, however, has not played out as smoothly as the Republican operators would have hoped, due to the entry of Donald Trump into the election cycle. Despite his businessman credentials, Trump's positions clashed entirely with the sort of economic framework promoted by the Tea Party's financial backers. His disavowal of free-trade agreements like NAFTA and the more recent Trans-Pacific Partnership, itself a curious mirror-image of the left, appears as a larger disavowal of the corporate internationalism that is one of the hallmarks of neoliberalism. His brand of *national capitalism,* cultivated to capture the disenfranchised middle class that was previously the Tea Party's support base, resurrects the notions of tariffs and exit-taxes to throw the break on globalizing processes. That so many who previously appeared as embracing *laissez-faire* attitudes towards trade are now embracing more traditionally populist visions illustrates that despite the attempted compact between the Republican financiers and the establishment and the so-called "silent majority," there existed a gap between the establishment and the constituency. This is reinforced by the long-time Tea Party talking point of privatizing Social Security and Medicare – a proposition that even at the time seemed out of touch with the self-proclaimed Tea Party grassroots. Unsurprisingly, Donald Trump has rejected the notion of turning these functions over the market.

To what extent can we say that Trump has actually stolen the momentum from the grassroots right of the Tea Party? We can note that several prominent figures in the Tea Party movement have recently given their support for Trump.[59] For example, Debbie Dooley, a board member of the Tea Party Patriots and one of the organizers of the first Tea Party protest, has declared that: "At a time when other candidates stood with Wall Street, Trump stood with Main Street and for American jobs. He strongly believes in American exceptionalism and will put American interests first." In a similar vein, Sarah Palin, former darling of the Tea Party movement and neoconservatives alike, has appeared at Trump rallies to rail at the "status quo" of each party's establishment. Incidences like these help reinforce the image Trump has constructed: as the political outsider, the rebel against the establishment – which was precisely the mantle held by the Tea Party only a handful of years earlier. While the Tea Party's rebellious image was one that actually doubled down on neoliberalism, the image that Trump projects is one that goes completely against it.

Besides the courting of Tea Party icons like Dooley and Palin, Trump's right-populist rhetoric taps directly into one of the central concerns of the Tea Party grassroots: the issue of immigration. While in its initial wave the Tea Party had focused itself on economic issues and opposing "big government," by 2013 the attitude had shifted towards an anti-immigration stance motivated by President Obama's proposed amnesty bill. This must be contextualized in the stagnant job growth of the years immediately following the recession (as discussed in the previous chapter), which lent itself to ethnic and racial scapegoating – one of the most notorious of which is the "job-stealing Mexican" trope. It was at this point that the establishment leadership of the Tea Party began to split with the grassroots leadership, with organizations such as the Koch-funded Americans for Tax Reform throwing their support to the amnesty bill while the regional Tea Party groups vigorously opposed it. To quote the founder of the Tea Party Nation in 2013, "The anger is more intense than it was in 2010. They are more upset about the amnesty bill than they were about Obamacare."[60] The bombastic declarations coming from Trump early in the campaign – the designation of immigrants as drug addicts and rapists, the plans to build a wall between the US and Mexico (that Mexico would pay for!), the conflation of immigration with the threat of Islamic fundamentalism – all served to tap directly into this wellspring of nationalist discontent.

The xenophobia stoked by Trump creates a political situation in the US that mirrors that of Europe, though perhaps to a lesser degree. Just as white nationalism and white power groups have seen a surge in the time since Trump's campaign began,[61] a wave of anti-immigrant and pro-nationalist sentiment has swept across Europe, posing a threat to the continued hegemony of the European Union. This has consistently been rising since the onslaught of the Great Recession (best exemplified, perhaps, by the rise of the Golden Dawn in Greece), but has gained considerable momentum as refugees have poured across the borders, fleeing from the humanitarian crisis in the Middle East. Terrorist attacks in Paris and Brussels have effectively poured gasoline on the fire – but the flames have been fanned by an increasingly powerful and vocal far-right.

At both home and abroad, this scenario poses a crisis for the neoliberal establishment. In the US, the growing momentum behind Trump threatens to overwhelm the candidates supporting the Washington Consensus. One by one they have dropped out of the race; both Paul and Rubio suffered heavy losses to Trump, with Cruz emerging as the establishment candidate of choice. This is surprising in and of itself, as in any other "normal" election cycle the presence of Cruz – and the host of regressive social and fiscal policies he proposes – would be scorned and derided. Yet the Koch Brothers and other conservative financiers have poured money into the Cruz campaign, into anti-Trump ads, and into ads against Republican competitor John Kasich.

While at the time that this is being written it remains to be seen which side in this struggle will win out, the long-term fallout from these events is all but certain. A Trump victory will strengthen his support base – while a Trump loss will undoubtedly rally more to the populist right. In either scenario, the Republican Party will be fundamentally altered; the relationship between the party's establishment and the party's base has shifted considerably, which will in turn flavor the approaches to economic, military, and social policies in the future. As the subterranean movement from the Tea Party to Trump shows, in times of crisis the discontent of the population does not dissipate – it merely takes on new forms in new contexts. It appears that this mutability can fracture even the most entrenched of political consensuses.

An identical scenario has played out on the side of the

Democratic Party, with the showdown between Hillary Clinton, the undeniable establishment favorite, and Bernie Sanders, a long-time senator who has consistently played the role of the political outsider. If Trump is the figurehead for the rising-tide of right-wing populism, Sanders is the same for left-wing populism. Trump's momentum was inadvertently laid years ago with the Tea Party; Sanders, likewise, appears to be carrying on the mantle of the Occupy movement. The rhetoric of Sanders draws heavily on the political priorities of Occupy, with his emphasizing of widening income inequality, the issue of money's corrosive influence in politics, and the question of mounting levels of debt. And just as Occupy appeared as a grassroots insurgency, the Sanders campaign presents itself as a "political revolution" pushed onward by radicalized segments of the population itself; disavowals of political action committees and the limiting of campaign contributions to individual donations reinforces this notion that civil society is injecting itself back into the political process.

Indeed, during Occupy's initial run in 2011, Sanders was perhaps the most vocal supporter of the movement in the government. To quote Sanders during the initial wave of the movement: "[Occupy is] speaking to the real anger and frustration that millions of Americans feel at a time when the middle class is collapsing, poverty is increasing, the people on top are doing phenomenally well."[62] Today, that support is being paid back with organizations such as The People for Bernie, a coalition that works closely with the Sanders campaign in helping coordinate action at the grassroots level. The two primary founders of The People for Bernie – Charles Lenchner and Winnie Wong – were central organizers and activists in the Occupy movement, and shortly thereafter launched a movement calling on Elizabeth Warren (the progressive legal scholar turned senator and early supporter of Occupy) to run for president. The strategy of this push would lay the foundation of The People for

Bernie – but as Wong is quick to point out, the ultimate goal is not to simply channel radical energy into a political campaign. "I like Bernie as a person very much," she said in an interview. "I consider him to be my brother and my organizing comrade. But I don't actually care that much about him. There is no frenzy around Bernie. I care about the participation of people."[63]

While the relationship between the ambition of the socialist left and the reformist left will be the topic of the following chapter, we should note that the reformist populism of Sanders deviates from the establishment reformism of, say, Obama (and that of Clinton). Sanders, like Trump on the right, seeks to break the party away from the tenets of neoliberalism. Like Trump, Sanders is suspicious of free-trade policies that offload labor into low-wage regions – though Sanders does not appeal to the same xenophobia and nationalist sentiment that Trump taps into. If anything, the so-called "socialism" of Sanders calls back to the liberal policies in the "golden age" of capitalism": the highly-regulated, highly-taxed, socially-conscious political and economic consensus that prevailed in the postwar years and across the 1950s and 1960s. Besides nods to the "Nordic Model" of social democracy, the exemplary figures of Sanders' "democratic socialism" include Presidents Franklin Roosevelt, John F. Kennedy, and Lyndon Johnson. Swimming in similar currents are some of his policy recommendations: jobs programs, increased investments in green energy and technology, subsidized education, universal healthcare, etc.

Thus we can see that just as the Republican Party's establishment has become estranged from much of its base, so too has the Democratic Party. In other words: while the party's establishment has held the line on the Washington Consensus, a large portion of those who identify as Democrats – or would be willing to throw their support behind the Democrats – are drifting further to the left. This is not only part of the overall breakdown of the Washington Consensus itself, but indicates the failure of long-term Democratic strategy. As we saw early, the party in the Reagan era redefined itself as one committed to business development; part and parcel of this attempt was the courting of the "Atari Democrats," that is, young liberals affiliated with the tech industry.[64] While this strategy unfolded in the 1980s, its legacy reverberates today, as Clinton has surpassed all other "candidates from both parties in individual donations from employees at the ten highest-grossing companies in Silicon Valley, including Google, Facebook, Apple, and eBay."[65] Sanders, by contrast, draws his support elsewhere, primarily from the moribund manufacturing and service industries, from minorities, and from retirees and students. Unsurprisingly, these were some of the groups hit the hardest during the recession – and a similar pattern can be found in the Trump support base, a large portion of which draws from the blue-collar labor force of the decimated manufacturing sector.[66]

The rise of left-wing economic populism, like the parallel increase in right-wing populism, is not limited to the United States alone. In Great Britain, where the Labour Party has played a role modeled on that of the US Democratic Party, Jeremy Corbyn has risen to leadership of the party's left-wing opposition faction. Running on an anti-austerity platform, Corbyn's support comes largely from the country's trade-union movement, themselves having been decimated since the days of Thatcher. Similarly, left-wing governments hold power in both Spain and Greece – though in the case of the latter, power is fragile given the repeated attempts of the European Union to stymie bids for economic autonomy. If 2011 was the year that dissenting segments of civil society struck out to reject the neoliberal vision of the future, the events of 2015 and 2016 mark the *structuralization* of these tendencies. Yet while neoliberalism has revealed itself to be a structuralizing agent par excellence, there is always something left over, something that evades the logic of neoliberalism.

We must stress again that there is no guarantee that the leftist tendency will go so far as to break the chains of neoliberalism, and in the US (at the time this is being written), losses on the part of the Sanders campaign continue to mount. Right-populism, embodied by Trump, still surges forward, but it remains to be seen how – and if – it would ultimately deviate from neoliberalism in practice. The most important aspect of all this to keep in mind, however, is that not all radiates from the offices of the politicians. Whether or not a given politician becomes the new figurehead or breaks the mold, it is the activities in the diffused networks of civil society that are the most important. If they no longer hold the line of the Washington Consensus (which seems very apparent at this moment), future manifestations of political action will reflect this, regardless of how the current election cycle works itself out. Movements do not pivot on the activities of the political class alone.

Chapter 3

Looking Forward

The Double Movement

"For a century," Karl Polanyi wrote in his 1944 masterpiece *The Great Transformation*, "the dynamics of modern society was governed by a double movement: the market expanded continuously but this movement was met by a countermovement checking the expansion in definite directions."[1] In his broad historical sweep, Polanyi had found that capitalism, emerging from the transformation of land and labor into commodities, sought to always dis-embed itself from society; that is, capitalism promoted an image of the market free from social regulation. We saw early in the previous chapter that this was precisely the vision offered by the early neoliberals, from the Austrian School to the Chicago School. By dis-embedding itself from social regulation, capitalism in its most unrestrained form becomes itself the mechanism that regulates society. Such is the structure hidden behind even the noblest rhetoric of *laissez-faire*, which ridiculously offers unbound marketization as the "voluntary exchange between sovereign individuals." Writing on the other side of the Great Depression, Polanyi found that this myth, one already tired by his time, had reigned over an increasingly globalized society between 1813 and 1914. This was the so-called "100-year peace" (as if the long depression, kicking off 1879, and the wave of colonialism that brought it to an apparent resolution constituted peace!), which came to its calamitous end in the outbreak of World War I, the Soviet Revolution, the rise of fascism in Europe, the Great Depression, and ultimately, for the United States, the anti-*laissez-faire* measures of the New Deal and the outbreak of the Second World War.

For as much as the market seeks to surpass society and bundle its relationships within its own matrices, society will come more and more to reject and resist this transformation. This is the double movement: the pendulum-like swings between the quest for unbridled marketization and the attempts to push it back. The movement is a constant in capitalist societies, but it appears that when the specter of crisis emerges on the horizon, with the precipitating rises in income inequality and falls in profit, that it begins to break through. We should follow Polanyi's suggestion and see that this end of the double movement, this *self-protection of society*, cuts both ways. It can appear in both left-wing and right-wing forms (and all manners in between), as socialism or fascism, egalitarianism or barbarism. The Soviet state in Russia, the fascist states in Italy and Germany, and the social-democratic state in New Deal-era America all appear as variations, in Polanyi's estimation, of the self-protection of society.

Is this not a perfect description of our own moment in time, in both the United States and abroad? At the time of this writing the rise of the fascist impulse is all too apparent, couched in the classical, yet unholy, marriage of racism, xenophobia, sexism, and nationalism with economic populism. Alongside the rise of Trump and Cruz through the political process, it can be witnessed in the increased visibility of white supremacist groups and militias, the attacks on immigrants and Muslims, and the brutal repression of inner-city blacks by a militarized police apparatus. Faced with existential crisis with no apparent resolution, the reactionaries form walls between their understanding of society and those they deem to be beyond it; they scapegoat and assault, turn their eyes away from those shot down in the streets and hurl insults to those who fight against it. All the while they may disavow their racism, their xenophobia, appealing instead to their common devotion to a nationalist myth of past greatness, embodied in the specter of the strong man. Indeed, studies have shown that support for Trump pivots not on religious affiliation, gender, age, economic level, or other stratification – but on support for authoritarianism.[2] One does not, however, need to read sociological studies to come to this conclusion. One only needs to encounter the supporters in their day-to-day lives.

Ultimately, it does not matter whether or not Trump is the authoritarian he presents himself as. Figures like Trump or Cruz are only symptoms of an underlying problem: the systemic fascist impulse lurking in the heart of our societies, which emerges to the surface during times of profound crisis. Fascism is latent in all capitalist societies, necessitating as they do the strong state, the military regime, the colonial administrator, etc., yet it is particularly true for American society. For all those who speak of volunteerism and consent as the building blocks of American capitalism, it would do well for them to be reminded that its engine of growth was built upon the slavery of blacks and the political marginalization of the poor, and that it took the ruthless expropriation and parceling out of land to maintain its rates of accumulation. The celebration of "civilized progress," enshrined by the United States as "Manifest Destiny," is a mystification of the bloody reality of the state and capital.

On a more institutional level, the fascist impulse is equally – if not even more – apparent. Producerism, a perversion of working-class consciousness that holds that those both at the top and bottom of the economic ladder are parasites sucking from the neck of labor, has long held sway in the United States; scratching the surface of this ideology will quickly reveal that its solidarity is limited to the white petty-bourgeoisie. "The sense of being cheated," writes Bruce Berlet, "undergrids the producerist worldview, and provides a powerful mobilizing framework for right-wing populism."[3] Berlet sees the producerist ideology as implicit in the classical Jacksonian tendency, with its simultaneous privileging of the "common working man" and oppression of blacks and Native Americans, while later iterations would include the overtly fascist followers of Father Coughlin and the idiosyncratic blending of the left and right by Louisiana governor Huey Long during the Great Depression. Through producerism, elements of left-wing populism – such as redistributive programs and protectionist trade policies – filter themselves through nativism, making it not only a threat to society as a whole but to any prospective left-wing movement.

In our contemporary era, this hybrid ideology found itself galvanized by the shift from industrial-monopoly capitalism to finance-monopoly capitalism and globalization. Rejection of NAFTA and other free-trade deals became the centerpiece of political movements such as the Reform Party of the United States, launched in 1995 by Ross Perot. Amongst its members were the so-called "prophet of protectionism" Pat Buchanan, a notorious racist and anti-Semite; David Duke, the former Grand Wizard of the Ku Klux Klan; and, in a strangely forgotten twist of history, Donald Trump. Though Trump would exit the Reform Party in 2000, citing irreconcilable political differences with "a Klansman, Mr. Duke, [and] a neo-Nazi, Mr. Buchanan,"[4] we have seen, some sixteen years later, Duke heartily endorse Trump and Buchanan declare that the mogul is "the future of the Republican Party."[5]

Rhetoric espoused by the likes of the Reform Party and others in the producerist current appeals directly to a middle class which finds itself dissolving away in the velocity of capitalism's flows. The denunciation of "welfare queens" and "job-stealing Mexicans," alongside "big government liberalism" and its regime of taxation, reflect the aimlessness of its analyses and the inherent violence of its logic. Its skepticism towards free trade leads it to positions that might resemble the left (Buchanan, for example, has readily adapted the language of grassroots leftist movements, castigating the 1%, high corporate salaries, and the outsourcing of jobs to low-wage countries),[6] while its adoration of power and the nation situate it squarely on the right. This does not mean that the producerist perspective cannot be redirected towards *laissez-faire* ends: after the Reform Party, the largest explosion of right-wing populism came in the form of the Tea Party, which struck a more economically libertarian chord. Yet as we reviewed in Chapter 2, the support of the Tea Party came from a middle class legitimately frustrated with declines in their standards of living. Thus the Austrian-libertarian perspective of the Tea Party is shrouded in irony: the solution proposed to their woes, which in reality emerged from capitalism itself, was to accelerate the processes of capitalism *beyond* the actually-existing conditions of neoliberalism. The large support for closed borders, alongside other protectionist measures, that could be found in the Tea Party base indicated, however, a disconnection between the movement at the grassroots level and their leadership.

At the same time, the gulf between the Austrian-libertarian (as advocated by Ron Paul and his followers) and the right-producerist perspective (as advocated by Buchanan and his coterie) is not as wide as it may initially appear. During the early 90s, the faction of the American libertarian movement centered on Llewelyn Rockwell (the long-time right-hand man for Paul) and Murray Rothbard (the protégé of proto-neoliberal scion Ludwig von Mises) sought an alliance with Buchanan's "Old Right"-style conservatism, a hybridization that was dubbed by Rockwell as "paleolibertarianism." This was, in short, the fusion of market libertarianism with social conservatism to preserve what was seen as a Western civilization decaying through progress and globalization. "Pornographic photography, 'free'-thinking, chaotic painting, atonal music, deconstructionist literature, Bauhaus architecture, and modernist film," wrote Rockwell in the paleolibertarian manifesto, "have nothing in common with the libertarian political agenda – no matter how much individual libertarians may revel in them... We obey, and ought to obey, traditions of manners and taste."[7] In "Right-Wing Populism: A Strategy for the Paleo Movement," Rothbard praised David Duke ("there was nothing in Duke's current program or campaign that could not also be embraced by paleoconservatives or paleo-libertarians"), while elsewhere voicing support for Buchanan.[8] "With Pat Buchanan as our leader," he declared in 1992, "we shall break the clock of social democracy... We shall repeal the twentieth century."[9] It is perhaps with these developments, which took place on the fringe of American politics, that the seeds of the current direction of right-wing producerism were formed, with Trump taking the mantle and far surpassing the ultimately doomed attempts of Buchanan.

We should not necessarily bog ourselves down with the detailed history of these turns (at least in these pages), for while they are dangerous in and of themselves, it is their evolution in the context of a wider turn towards the right that truly matters. They are, at best, a basic infrastructure for the emergent fascist expression of the self-protection of society. This infrastructure, in turn, lends itself to the *institutional adaptation* that must take place during each period of acute capitalist crisis. Hence the rise of fascism, in a language even more overt and vitriolic than that found in the United States, in Europe. Just as right-producerism has inevitably emerged from the crisis of the capitalism and the breakdown of the American political system in the US, European fascism takes aim at the European Union for its consistent failures in alleviating the deconstruction of daily life. And just as those in America rail against immigrants crossing the southern border, the European right unleashes itself against the waves of refugees entering the continent from the war-torn Middle East. That it was the West's own geopolitical maneuvers that dissolved the Middle East and set the conditions for the refugee crisis is lost on (or more accurately, willfully ignored by) the European fascist, just as the American fascist pays little heed to the ongoing dismantling of the global south by the north.

Fascism is nothing less than the intensification of every regressive sentiment to be found in the whole of society, mobilized and put on the march by elements in the ruling class. As Rajani Dutt noted, the exclusionary logic of fascism "is the art of playing on the hopes and fears, the emotions and ignorance of the poor and the suffering for the benefit of the rich and powerful."[10] Fascism emerges on the foundations of the existing order, and may even appear as the final solution to the crisis of this order. This occurs, naturally, following the dismantling of all other alternatives to the existing order, which is precisely what the order must have done to advance itself. This is why American has such a propensity for the fascist impulse: it has waged an aggressive conflict against anything that resembles a movement of the workers, of the self-recognition of the proletarian condition. This has not been unique to the neoliberal era, but has existed as a near-constant thread through the whole of America history. In the wake of the Second World War, for example, social scientists turned to the vexing problem of fascism and looked for ways to prevent its gesticulation within American society. Just as Keynesian economics approaches the crisis of capitalism the way a mechanic might fix a broken car, these social scientists approached society the way a psychologist would approach one afflicted with mental illness. For them, the impulse for fascism emerged from a lack of communication and a lack of opportunity; they proposed in equal and interrelated turns the creation of democratic media, cultural acceptance and education, and a "People's Capitalism."[11] Thus the solution for fascism, in the context of the postwar boom, became indistinguishable from Keynesianism itself – yet the question of the worker, of the fundamentally exploitative dimensions of the division of labor, went unaddressed. This opened the door for the anti-worker counterrevolution. In other words, the innate failure of American social democracy *provided the very conditions for the rise of neoliberalism.*

This is the reality of the insurgent fascist impulse tearing through American society at large today: it is the result of two failures, the general and inevitable failure of the capitalist mode of production and the failure of social democracy to advance itself beyond capitalism. We can see the rocky relationship between Polanyi's self-protection of society and the class struggle, in that the rise of both social democracy and fascism can serve to stabilize capitalism through providing a framework for institutional adaptation. Both seek a harmonization of classes and a maintaining of the fundamental aspects of the capitalist organization of production. This is not to say, of course, that social democracy and fascism are identical currents. Both are solutions to a crisis that are diametrically opposed to one another, even if social democracy can lend form to fascism down the road.

If the ascendency of Trump is the latest tendency in the right-populist expression of society's self-protection that first gained traction with the Tea Party, the social-democratic expression embodied by Bernie Sanders can be traced to the leftist self-expression of society that we can pinpoint as starting during the presidential campaign of Barack Obama. A point of clarification: what we mean by this is that the push for a progressive president, one with a pedigree in organizing and community action, is evidence of the self-protection of society, not the neoliberal reality of Obama. It follows, accordingly, that the cohesiveness of this self-protection took higher form in the Occupy movement, being attributable in part to the failure of Obama to fulfill the progressive image that he offered. As we argued in the previous chapter, the rhetoric of Sanders, along with his current support base, built upon the events of 2011.

One must ask to what degree these developments are indicative of swelling class struggle. There is a strong argument to be had that they are, albeit in an extremely underdeveloped form. This is indicated by the paradoxes and contradictions that plague this tendency. In the support for Obama, for example, we can see the near-abandoning in class consciousness of the belief that radical change can come from the center of the Democratic establishment, much less the Oval Office. The radicalism of

Occupy appeared far beyond that of the support for Sanders, yet it too was marred by contradictions. By and large, the political orientation of Occupy marked an underdevelopment in class consciousness in that its aims were simply a regulation of Wall Street and a higher tax rate for the wealthy. At the same time, the decentralized organizational structure of Occupy indicated the embrace of more anarchic energies, found most specifically in its extreme horizontalism and consensus-based decision-making processes. The movement that was Occupy, in other words, operated beyond its own logic. This is not to say that its latent anarchism was without problems, as it posed as many limitations to itself as passages forward.

Perhaps the more revolutionary movement to emerge in recent years has been Black Lives Matter, taking aim at the racist regime that upholds the organization of production. The antagonism to the dominant order that the movement has displayed has been powerful and invigorating, and sends a message to the rest of the left as it does to the police and the politicians. This is a message that transcends the self-imposed limitations of social democracy, and speaks directly to the necessity of direct action in the face of oppression. Furthermore, it highlights that the reality of the so-called "conscious capitalism" that came into being in the 1990s – which arguably has seduced many even on the radical left[12] – is a mystification of intensified racial violence and exclusionary social, political, and economic practices. Without building and strengthening constructive alliances with these movements, the broader revitalized left will find difficulties moving beyond liberalism, and thus be significantly weakened in the face of rising fascism.

This brings us now to the question of Sanders. There is no doubt that his "socialism" (or even his "democratic socialism", as he calls it) falls far from the central tenets of socialism, and strictly within the context of social democracy. Instead of challenging the modes of production, he seeks to maintain them, albeit with a kinder, gentler face. Instead of marshalling class forces to break with capitalism, he hopes to re-integrate those marginalized by the organization of production and the so-called "democratic processes" of the United States in order to return it to optimal efficiency. We can hear echoes of the words of the German Social Democratic Party in 1931: "We must be the physicians of ailing capitalism."[13] Historical analogy is, of course, shaky at best, and it must be stressed that the material conditions of today are quite different than those of the 1930s, even if we find ourselves in the aftermath of economic crisis and facing the rise of the right. The sins of the GSPD have caused generations of socialists to be wary of social democracy, and given the trajectory of contemporary American history, it would appear that they would be correct. Yet much has changed since the 1930s, and even from the 1960s, which is precisely what we must keep in mind.

Sanders and Socialism

The Keynesian Question

The majority of the positions that Sanders espouses, like the European social democracies that he points to, stem from Keynesian economics: redistribution taking place through taxation in order to boost consumer purchasing power, the funding of public works as a means to job growth, the restraining of capitalism's excesses, so on and so forth. This leads Sanders to consistently invoke the "golden age" of capitalism, the period running from the New Deal to around 1968, as evidence that these policies work in a way that is both economically feasible and beneficial to society (particularly for those at the bottom). As reviewed in the first chapter, however, the golden age of growth could only be contextualized in the conditions created by World War II; namely, the transformation of the United States into global hegemon based on strong manufacturing, export-oriented industrialization, and the position of the dollar as the international reserve currency. We should not say that the utilization of Keynesian economics did not aid the postwar economic arrangement (it absolutely did!), but it seems doubtful that such a high rate of growth could have occurred without the massive amounts of capital (particularly constant capital, as in buildings, equipment, and critical infrastructures) that had been destroyed in the global conflict.

Regardless, the Keynesian consensus that took shape in this time molded the outlook of contemporary Marxist economists, best indicated by the increased presence of Keynes in the *Monthly Review* School associated with Paul Baran and Paul Sweezy. The pro-Keynesian Marxists generally subscribed to the underconsumption variant of crisis theory, holding that the tendency to expel workers from production or maintain worker's wages at a low rate would play limitations on how much surplus could be absorbed. As we saw in Chapter 1, however, underconsumption is a specter that haunts capitalism throughout the entirety of its run, and it is only in periods of sweeping transformation (the introduction of paradigm-shifting innovations, or a sharp decline in the rate of profit) that underconsumption exacerbates and adds to pre-existing distortions in the economy. Thus while underconsumption plays a vital role in the coming into being of a crisis, it is by no means the roots cause; it is instead a symptom of the underlying sets of contradictions. From this perspective, Keynesian solutions to the crises of capitalism, building directly upon lifting up consumption levels through policies of full employment, appear inadequate to do anything other than apply a band-aid that could only last temporarily.

Furthermore, we must take account of the feasibility of pursuing full employment policies under capitalism in the long term. Marx argues that capitalism inherently generates what he calls the "reserve army of the unemployed," that is, the large pool of unemployed (and perhaps underemployed) that exists alongside those who find steady work. The instant objection, at first, is that it seems short-sighted to claim this state of affairs as an inevitability; after all, is this not precisely where general underconsumption comes from? As a response, let us take into consideration what would happen under a hypothetical state of full employment. As the need for workers to compete with one another would decline, owners would be forced into the position of competing for workers through increasing the price of wages offered, particularly where skilled workers are concerned. In this worker-dominated market, workers would also maintain the upper hand in bargaining for other benefits, unionization, pro-labor contracts and the like, which would result, if we take the entirety of the economy in aggregate, in the declining profits flowing to the owners. The realization of surplus value, in other words, would slow and stagnate. This is precisely the reason for the consistent state of medium to high rates of unemployment and underemployment: to continually expand the rate of surplus-value realization and to prevent the gaining of power by the working class. Indeed, as Keynesian Marxist economist Michal Kalecki (himself affiliated with the *Monthly Review* School) argued, full-employment policies would be temporary and usually occur during periods of peak profitability; as profits fall political battles will be waged to strip away these full-employment policies.[14] Given that Kalecki made these observations in the early 1940s, it seems that the events of the 1970s – and the entire neoliberal paradigm that followed – left his arguments completely vindicated. This brings us, once again, to the problem of social democracy itself.

Does this mean that we reject Keynesian policies outright? Absolutely not! To quote Costas Lapavistas, "Keynes and Keynesianism, unfortunately, remain the most powerful tools we've got, even as Marxists, for dealing with issues of policy in the here and now."[15] What we should do is juxtapose two different kinds of Keynesianism, a major (or right-wing) and minor (or left-wing) Keynesianism, if you will. The major Keynesianism is the establishment Keynesianism of the postwar consensus (and of people such as Paul Krugman today): the Keynesianism of trade and fiscal policy and as container of class struggle. A minor Keynesianism, on the other hand, is a Keynesianism of *strategy* that seeks to strengthen the working class in terms of political position and economic grounding. There is without a doubt a slippage between a major and minor Keynesianism, yet given the denigrated state of the class struggle today, it may very well be the only way to make headway. To quote Kalecki:

Labour must have no illusions about the great fight that will have to be waged against these [capitalist interest] groups. They will resist fiercely because what is at stake is not so much their profits as their personal and social power, which takes two forms: power in society as a whole, and power over workers' industry. As long as the first form of power remains, all the efforts of the workers in the factories and through the trade unions to diminish the second form of power can only have limited success. The fight for workers' rights in industry and for more effective workers' representation through such things as works' councils and production committees is, of course, of very great importance and... it has a vital part to play in the total *struggle against the capitalists. But it can never be a* substitute *for the necessary political fight to destroy the power wielded over society as a whole by the great capitalist interest-groups.*[16]

Could a Keynesian policy, even in minor form, possibly make a dent in the extreme inequality we're witnessing today, and stem the tide of the protracted crisis? As we've reviewed already, upswings that counteract the tendency of the rate of profit to fall occur following the introduction of new rounds of innovations that allow for investments to flow freely. This requires, of course, a precipitating expansion of surplus value that is realized in the form of profit. There have been suggestions that the sluggish recovery from the Great Recession, with its low rate of investments, is due to the problem posed by Baran and Sweezy: that monopoly capitalism stagnates because profits outpace the number of possible investment outlets. In other words, the number of innovations (paradigm-shifting or otherwise) would be minor compared to the "wall of capital" that is held by corporations. This appears to us to be an erroneous proposition, as during this period of recession *countless innovations have accumulated*. In the realm of paradigm shifts, the most obvious of innovations is the advancements carried out in green technology. These include not only eco-friendly automobiles, new agricultural techniques, efficient wind, solar, and geothermal energy technology, batteries, etc. – yet the global total of investments into green technology has remained marginal in the face of other investment and, more importantly, the accumulation of fictitious capital in finance. Without a sweeping reconfiguration of the flows of capital itself, the gap between the stagnation of the now and the unleashing of the productive potential in these innovations will only lengthen.

Co-Op Capitalism and Market Socialism

One aspect of Sander's economic philosophy that has consistently moved under the radar has been his support for worker-owned co-operatives as an alternative to the top-down autocratic model of "corporate capitalism." In his December 2014 "An Economic Agenda for America," he argued that "Instead of giving huge tax breaks to corporations which ship our jobs to China and other low-wage countries, we need to provide assistance to workers who want to purchase their own businesses by establishing worker-owned cooperatives."[17] Similar proposals have been made by Jeremy Corbyn in Great Britain, having told the Co-Operative Party in a 2015 address that "I believe in public ownership, but I have never favoured the remote nationalised model that prevailed in the postwar era... I want to give employees a statutory right to request employee ownership during business succession, and to tenants to demand the same if their landlord decides to sell multiple properties."[18]

Worker self-managed co-operatives have a long history in socialist thought, being particularly prominent in the more anarchic tendencies such as mutualism and syndicalism. At first blush, they seem to fulfill the basic tenet of socialist thought – the worker ownership of the means of production – yet what we are concerned with here is their application in an otherwise market-based system. An entire school of thought, *market socialism*, has co-existed alongside Marxist tendencies for the entirety of its existence, taking on different forms throughout history. These include the decentralized markets advocated by Pierre-Joseph Proudhon (1809–1865), the American "Anarchist-Socialism" of Benjamin Tucker (1854–1939), Lenin's New Economy Policy (1921–1928) the application of neoclassical competition theories to socialist planning by Oskar Lange (1904–1965), Yugoslavia's deployment of worker self-management within a competitive market framework (1950s–early 1980s), and Vietnam's "socialist-oriented market economy" (1986 through present). Today, one of the more vocal proponents is economist Gar Alperovitz; his call for government support for community-owned business models is undoubtedly the key inspiration for Sander's own reflections.[19] It falls closely in line, furthermore, with the idea of the "Partner State" advanced by Jeremy Rifkin and the P2P Foundation's Michel Bauwens, a reformed state apparatus that assists civil society in "creating value" through the support for commons, peer production, co-operative ownership and free exchange.[20]

Many socialists might be suspicious of these developments, given that the market appears as the foundation of capitalist society and the mechanism through which it regulates the social. This is without a doubt true, but we must also keep in mind that markets are a means to allocate resources that have found their application in many places throughout history, in societies both capitalist and non-capitalist. The un-nuanced identification of capitalism and the market must be contested, and it would behoove fellow socialists to deeply consider the potential benefits of decentralized and small-batch production, particularly at points where peer-to-peer platforms and commons enter into dialogue. At the same time, a cautious optimism of either co-operative capitalism or market socialism must be maintained. In the world existing as it currently is, market socialism cannot be taken as a goal in and of itself if long-term transformation is what is pursued. At best, a "minor Keynesianism" can be pursued as a means of strengthening the working class through macroeconomic policy with market socialism playing a similar role at the microeconomic level.

What are the current limitations of market socialism? It is hard to see how the turn to market mechanisms as the coordinating system for socialist enterprise would not exhibit, in time, a slippage back towards *laissez-faire* capitalism – just as the implementation of Keynesianism would almost certainly be temporary and rolled back as soon as the opportunity presented itself. This is in keeping with the laws of motion of capitalism, which see reproduction taking through continual expansion of capital accumulation through competition between capitalist firms. This, of course, is precisely what leads to the tendency of the rate of profit to fall: as competition intensifies, it becomes harder to realize the high rates of profit, leading in turn to structural transformations in the way labor is carried out. This process will hold true for co-operatives as much as it does for any traditionally-organized capitalism firms. Forced to compete, the co-operative at some point will have to face the situation of cutting compensation levels for the worker-owners, the elimination of worker-owners from the payroll, and more than likely both of these situations. In these situations, the social regulation of the capitalist market becomes all too clear, forming an informal technique that structuralizes dissenting forces into the mirror of its own image.

An example of this would be the Mondragon Corporation, a federation of worker cooperatives in the Basque region of Spain. Evolving from co-operatives launched by Distributist Catholic priest José María Arizmendiarrieta in the early 1940s, Mondragon is regarded as the exemplar of worker self-owned models; by 2010, it had some 85,000 members, many of whom take part in administrative decision-making processes through annual general assemblies. Gender equality and other humanist policies direct the entire outlook of the Mondragon program, leading to overwhelming endorsements from progressives, anarchists, and Marxists alike. Yet Mondragon has not been immune to the corrosive effects of the global capitalist economy: in 1993, as the neoliberal paradigm shifted into high gear, the corporation introduced salary differentials, a more traditional model of CEOs and directorships, and a streamlined business-savvy perspective tooled for advertisements in *Fortune* magazine. In keeping with the phenomena of globalization, Mondragon took part in the purchasing of businesses and factories in countries sold off under IMF-enforced structural adjustment programs. While this perhaps provided an opportunity to broaden the scope of its co-operative model, it ultimately chose to recreate the fundamental exploitation inherent to global uneven development by barring these newly acquired workers from membership in the greater co-operative federation and decision processes.[21] In one case, the Mondragon-owned Polish firm Fagor Mastercook was located in a special economic zone with its workers subjected to sweatshop-level wages; when unions attempted to organize the workforce and demand higher pay, employees involved in organizing were fired and security guards were turned out against peaceful protestors. In cases such as these (Fagor Mastercook, incidentally, is not the only one), Mondragon appears as less an egalitarian co-operative than a once-progressive institution transforming itself into a full-fledged capitalist firm.

Another example that we can turn to is the extensive experimentation done with market-directed worker-owned co-operatives carried out by Yugoslavia under Tito, beginning with the country's break with the Soviet Union and the subsequent "de-Stalinization" that started in 1952. The shift from a top-heavy bureaucratic model to one of bottom-up socialism via free enterprise was seen as carrying out the historical process of the *withering away of the state*.[22] In order to ensure that workers were compensated through the accumulation of profits, tariffs were reduced and borders were opened. What the workers gained in terms of autonomy and self-direction (through the free creation of trade unions and worker's councils) was offset, however, by the opening of their economy to the ebbs and flows of the global economy. Regardless, the country's economy soared throughout the 1960s, outpacing the growth rates of many developed countries. In 1975 the World Bank declared that the "Yugoslav economic system has to be judged a success"[23] – but it was at this moment the wave crested and rolled back. As the global crisis of the 1970s set into full force, Yugoslavia was impacted heavily, triggering waves of lay-offs and increasing rates of income inequality. By the 1980s, the country's elite turned to stabilization measures offered by the IMF and World Bank, setting off a chain of events that would lead to the rigorous deconstruction of Yugoslavia's socialist orientation.

Joseph Stiglitz, former chief economist at the World Bank and a staunch critic of neoliberalism, charges that the failures of Yugoslavia, alongside other market-socialist countries (including Hungary and the Soviet Union under Gorbachev), stem not from their commitment to socialism, but to the economic models that underpinned their decentralization. These are the very same neoclassical models of "general equilibrium" – innovated by Walras and Pareto and built upon by Arrow and Debreu – that serve as the foundation of much of the current neoliberal consensus.[24] Stiglitz thus takes aim at the notion of the market as a self-organizing mechanism that, left to its own devices, does not "spread around the wealth" in the way that its most fervent adherents maintain. And to be fair, the contemporary co-op movement advanced by social democrats stems not from a neoclassical or neoliberal framework, but understands itself as operating within a renewed Keynesian framework. Our proposition is that a macroeconomics of Keynesianism and microeconomics of co-operativism, if taken in and of themselves without a wider transformation, will eventually slip back into a neoliberal modality. Whatever equilibrium this proposed synthesis will be shaken by the sheer forces of capitalism's laws of motion unfolding through historical time. They will suffer, in other words, from the limitations to reformist politics.

Reform and Revolution

In 1900 Rosa Luxemburg unleashed a vigorous attack on the Social Democrats of Germany and their chief theorist Eduard Berstein. In his revisionist take on Marxist theory, Bernstein advocated the "evolutionary" perspective of socialist development, alleging that socialism could arise through gradual changes and transformations within the structures of capitalism itself. Incremental reforms such as worker's right, wage increases and welfare programs would lead to a more "developed" capitalism that would organically transform itself into a socialist society. In its final form, Bernstein's evolutionary socialism saw little purpose in the final realization of socialism; for him, the path there was the only thing that mattered. Against this Luxemburg labelled Bernstein an idealist, one ignoring the historical nature of capitalism and the laws of motion that reverse any applied fixes before they accumulate to a transformative point. Acknowledging the inevitability of capitalist crisis, she argued that should *we examine the large factors of social development, we see that we are not moving toward an epoch marked by a victorious development of trade unions, but rather toward a time when the hardships of labour unions will increase. Once industrial development has attained its highest possible point and capitalism has entered its descending phase on the world market, the trade union struggle will become doubly difficult. In the first place, the objective conjuncture of the market will be less favourable to the sellers of labour power, because the demand for labour power will increase at a slower rate and labour supply more rapidly than at present. In the second place, the capitalists themselves, in order to make up for losses suffered on the world market, will make even greater efforts than at present to reduce the part of the total product going to the workers (in the form of wages). The reduction of wages is, as pointed out by Marx, one of the principal means of retarding the fall of profit. The situation in England already offers us a picture of the beginning of the second stage of trade union development. Trade union action is reduced of necessity to the simple defence of already realised gains, and even that is becoming more and more difficult. Such is the general trend of things in our society. The counterpart of this tendency should be the development of the political side of the class struggle.*[25]

The origins of the Bernstein-Luxemburg debate can be traced back to Marx and Engel's debate with the nascent German Social Democratic Party over their party platform, the Gotha Program, in 1875. Named for the town in which it was drafted, the Gotha Program had been heavily influenced by social reformer Ferdinand Lasalle, whom Marx had seen as a political opportunist riding on the wave of the worker's movement. A non-Marxist, Lasalle emerged at once to have supported many aspects of bourgeois society alongside the anarchic mutualism of Proudhon; as such, one of his key planks was state-aided worker co-operatives. These concerns were appealed to in the text of the Gotha Program, alongside demands for "fair distribution," "equal rights" for labor to take part in wealth, and a shortening of the work day.[26] Most importantly, it spoke of these reforms as the conditions to realize a "free state," effectively eschewing the socialist goal of the workers' revolution.

Taking aim at the language of "fair distribution," Marx countered that "Do not the bourgeoisie assert that the present-day distribution is fair? And is it not, in fact, the only 'fair' distribution on the basis of the present-day mode of production?"[27] In other words, the Gotha Program, by focusing on the distribution of goods, neglected the basic foundation of capitalist exploitation in the arrangement of production and the division of labor, and by extension, failed to see how it was this division that created the system of unequal distribution. Without addressing how production is managed, there is no litmus test for determining what constitutes "fair distribution" beyond that which the logic of the market determines it to be. This alone has powerful ramifications today, as it lends credence to the riposte offered by much of the capitalist class to the advocates of "fair trade" – that "free trade *is* fair trade." We certainly know that "free trade" is unequal and exploitative (unfair, if you will), but as long as those who advocate for "fair trade" do so on the basis of the capitalist system they have very little to stand upon. This, too, was at the heart of Marx's *Critique of the Gotha Program*: that the Social Democrats had little interest in moving beyond the capitalist system, and actually hoped to reinforce it in their vision of the "free state." In regards to their demand for a progressive income tax, for example, "Taxes are the economic basis of the government machinery and of nothing else. In the state of the future, existing in Switzerland, this demand has been pretty well fulfilled. Income tax presupposes various sources of income of the various social classes and hence capitalist society."[28]

The German Social Democratic Party replaced the Gotha Party in 1891 with the Erfurt Program, drafted with the input of Edward Bernstein and Karl Kautsky (one of the leading Marxist theoreticians of the time). The Erfurt Program took a far more anti-capitalist stance than its predecessor, bringing into view the Marxist approach to crisis theory as a counterpoint to the idea of an egalitarian balance between classes. "The gulf between the propertied and the propertyless," reads the Erfurt Program, "is further widened by crises that are grounded in the nature of the capitalist mode of production, crises that are becoming more extensive and more devastating, that elevate this general uncertainty into the normal state of society and furnish proof that the powers of productivity have grown beyond society's control, that the private ownership of the means of production has become incompatible with their appropriate application and full development."[29] Yet it was Bernstein who would come to reject the Marxist theories of crisis by the late 1890s. If capitalism suffered from contradictions, he seemed to suggest, they would organically smooth themselves out as the system reached higher stages of development.

The time that Bernstein was writing these thoughts correlated to the magnificent rise of monopoly capitalism, and the bolstering of the centralized cartels through imperialism and financialization. For many, the appearance of an economy strengthening seemed to counteract Marx's argument that capitalism would tend towards crisis; for example, Rudolf Hilferding, an economist associated with both the German Social Democratic Party and the Social Democratic Party of Austria, posed the novel solution that it was monopolization and financialization, not crisis and revolution, that showed the way out from capitalism. "The socializing function of finance capital facilitates enormously the task of overcoming capitalism," he posited. "Once finance capital has brought the most importance branches of production under its control, it is enough for society, through its conscious executive organ – the state conquered by the working class – to seize finance capital in order to gain immediate control of these branches of production."[30] The fatal conceit of Hilferding's position was that financialization was an indicator of industry shoring itself up against and transcending the ups and downs of the business cycle – just as the fatal conceit of this wider revisionism was that capitalism would develop linearly over time, organizing itself to the point in which a smattering of reforms would usher in the realization of socialism. That revolution, World War, and extreme global crisis would tear through the world a handful of years later illustrates clearly the faulty logic of these propositions.

Why bother rehearsing these historical turns, now well over a century old? It is because that we feel that the "orthodox" Marxists have a wider historical scope, and a deeper under-standing of the laws of motion of capitalism, than their revisionist brethren. Furthermore, though the capitalist mode of production has transformed and re-organized itself on a global level, its basic laws and tendencies still go unchanged, thus making the problems facing reform today the same as before. The gambit of reform, in other words, will be doomed if it takes itself as the central goal of revolutionary behavior. Yet the *gambit of reform will remain just that if the question of crisis is not addressed in full*. Regardless of whether the rate of profit falls in a secular manner or countervailing tendencies persist in lifting it back up repeatedly, the sharp declines exhibited in crisis – and the hyper-exploitation required to move beyond them – will continue to ravage it, as we saw in Chapter 1. This fundamental recognition was made not only by the Marxists, but the bourgeois economists as well. Case in point is the theory of Joseph Schumpeter, who came to the conclusion in his studies of "creative destruction" that socialism was unavoidable: "there is inherent in the capitalist system a tendency towards self-destruction," he wrote, one that would generate the conditions where "things and souls are transformed in such a way as to become increasingly amenable to the socialist way of life."[31]

It is this recognition, that capitalism is capable of undermining itself in the long run and creating the condition for its own negation to emerge internal to itself, that generates the movement from capitalism to fascism. Indeed, the seeds of fascism are planted the second that the prophets of the free market call upon the forces of law and order to uphold the "right" to private property, the division of labor, and the logic of exchange. The focus on law and order by the Austrian School, right at the beginning of the neoliberal project, was an explicit attempt to separate capitalism's motion from the demands of popular democracy – which explains how Ludwig von Mises, proclaimed by his flock to be an arbiter of democracy, came to denounce Italian fascism while simultaneously arguing that "It cannot be denied that Fascism and similar movements aiming at the establishment of dictatorships are full of the best intentions and their intervention has, for the moment, saved European civilization. The merit that Fascism has thereby won for itself will live on eternally in history."[32] It is in this same vein, though not in such a bombastic way, that Ron Paul was able to unleash his denunciations of democracy in the name of the "Republic."[33] And finally, it is reflected in the strange support amongst the ranks of the libertarians and the "anarcho-capitalists" for Trump in the US and neo-fascism in the EU. *It is the specter of the collapse of the capitalist consensus that weds capitalism and fascism together.*

It is for these reasons that we must say that reform is necessary at the present stage. This is not a call for all to become Sanders supporters (or Corbyn supporters), or to funnel vital critical energies into electoral campaigns. What it is a call for, however, is an intimate and enhanced engagement with the political processes on all scales of power: the immediate, the local, the regional, and the national. These scales run the gamut from neighborhood associations and community councils to city councils to broader political positions. It also means no longer rallying behind singular candidates who arise to approximate our views, but to become those candidates and figures of leaders.

It means building broad coalitions and forsaking sectarian divides.

The reader might see an immediate contradiction between this stance and the one that has been building through this chapter. Our contention is that while the critics of revisionism, such as Marx and Luxemburg, among others, are correct in their assessments that social democracy and reformism are ineffectual and ineffective on a historical scale, the material conditions of the present none-the-less demand that the full forces of reformism be brought to the fore to combat neoliberalism. Reform and revolution are not diametrically opposing systems, but are intricately bound together. *To reform capitalism, at this stage, is a revolutionary act*, though only a part of a wider revolutionary struggle. As outlined in the preceding sections of this book, the force that has been dubbed "neoliberalism" is a political manifestation of "crisis-response" in regards to a greater crisis of profitability. It has deconstructed the capabilities of the class struggle to piece through it, and has made significant strides by treating the hard-earned victories of previous class struggle as primitive accumulation for its own (rather stagnant) expansion.

The reality is that when the earlier debate over reform and revolution was raging the class struggle was considerably stronger. In Germany, the Social Democratic Party and their rivals, the Communist Party of Germany, constituted major political parties with broad and powerful support bases. Likewise, the Social Democratic Party of Austria was able to transform Vienna, for a brief period prior to the rise of fascism in Europe, into a socialist municipality.[34] In the United States, the Socialist Party of America enjoyed a large membership, and alongside organizations such as the Industrial Workers of the World was able to strengthen the nascent labor and trade-union movements. Eugene Debs, a leader in the Socialist Party, ran for president in 1912 and 1920, gaining over 900,000 votes in each run. And in Russia, of course, the revolution was capable of overturning the country's ruling class; despite the inarguable problems of the Soviet system, the USSR was able to aid and support socialist revolutionaries the world over.

Today, no such organized class struggle exists on a global, much less national level. The barrier to the struggle is neoliberalism (and its fascistic offspring), and it follows accordingly that neoliberalism must be rolled back if any struggle or movement is going to advance itself. Yes, the current situation does bear a curious historical resemblance to the conditions of the 1920s and 30s, but the dynamics of resistance – of social self-protection – have been radically transformed. In our laboring bodies we are far more isolated from one another and from production itself; in our time and our minds we are far more exhausted; in our leisure far more seduced; in our relationships far more atomized. We cannot be said to be precarious only in our economic situations, for precarity has pervaded every aspect of our daily lives: our social environment is as shattered as the capitalism that runs headlong through it. The growing fascist resentment is but a symptom of this wider problem.

Neoliberalism, in its bid to transform its citizen-subjects into the *homo econimus*, has attempted to rob us of that which can bring us together by blotting out the capacity to experience solidarity. This is both inadvertent and advertent, the byproduct of ruthless gutting of society under the declaration that "there is no alternative" and the hoisting upon us of a spectrum of techniques that tell us that it is a situation of *every person for theirs and their own*, that *wealth is there for the one who wants it*, and that *he who competes the most wins the most*. To overcome this most absurd state of affairs we must find a way to rekindle that capacity for solidarity on a grand scale, not only for worker struggles but for racial struggles, immigrant struggles, gender and sexual struggles, student struggles, environmental struggles – or, in other words, to reclaim a way to express humanity beyond the language of exchange and profits and quotas, and beyond the narrow and ridiculous understanding of humanity as framed by sexuality, gender, and borders.

The fountain of the human spirit cannot flow forth by state action. Even under a reformist paradigm, the state will still operate the same as it always has, as an "organ of class domination, the organ of oppression of one class by another."[35] Its goal remains the maintenance of "an order which legalizes and perpetuates this oppression by moderating the collision between classes." This goal does not change in the passage from the neoliberal state to a social-democratic state. That said, we believe that given the sheer denigration of the class struggle in today's world, socialists have no choice but to accelerate a reformist paradigm at all scales of political experience. By the same token, we urge non-socialist activists to understand the basic impossibility of long-term progressive reforms and class compromise in the face of capitalism's flows. Any reform, then, must consist of what Nick Srnicek and Alex Williams, following Andre Gorz, call "non-reformist reforms." As they write:

> By this we mean three things. First, they have a utopian edge that strains at the limits of what capitalism can concede. This transforms them from polite requests into insistent demands charged with belligerence and antagonism. Such demands combine the futural orientation of utopias with the immediate intervention of the demand, invoking a 'utopianism without apology'. Second, these reformist proposals are grounded in real tendencies of the world today, giving them a viability that revolutionary dreams lack. Third, and most importantly, such demands shift the political equilibrium and construct a platform for further development... The proposals... will not break us out of capitalism, but they do promise us a way out of neoliberalism, and to establish a new equilibrium of political, economic, and social forces.[36]

Srnicek and William's non-reformist reforms concern the

construction of "post-work imaginaries," based on the drive towards full automation, universal basic income, a shorter working week and a whittling away of the work ethic. Unfortunately, the question of "post-work" and automation is beyond the scope of these pages, but we agree with Srnicek and Williams that by establishing sets of future-oriented demands we can build up a counter-hegemony to the "there-is-no-alternative" mentality of neoliberalism. Breaking with neoliberalism would entail the strengthening of worker protections, the increase of wages, the broadening of welfare, the regulation of the economy, and the partial rolling back of the juridical order that has been designed to tear apart these democratic mechanisms. To break the back of neoliberalism means to lessen the grip that precarity has on our lives, and by extension, set into motion conditions equitable for the building of the broader movement.

Under such a much-needed scenario the needs of building the broad movement, integrated from all those struggling against oppression in any form, cannot be forsaken by the struggles for social democracy. The two must operate in syncopation, as a versatile opportunity structure, with the latter boosting and amplifying the possibility space constructed by the former. Every step forward in terms of the social democratic movement must advance the struggle beyond the limitations of social democracy; the two must overrun the dual pincers of economic and political denigration. Only in the proliferation of intersectional movements, co-operatives, mutual aid infrastructures, antifa (anti-fascist movements), agorism, etc. can social democracy mean anything other than a fleeting and momentary concession, a breath of air before being submerged again in the torrents of exploitation and marginalization. To draw an example from Marx's *Critique of the Gotha Program*:

> *That the workers desire to establish the conditions for co-operative*
> *production on a social scale, and first of all on a national scale, in*

their own country, only means that they are working to revolutionize the present conditions of production, and it has nothing in common with the foundation of co-operative societies with state aid. But as far as the present co-operative societies are concerned, they are of value only insofar as they are the independent creations of the workers and not proteges either of the governments or of the bourgeois.[37]

Social Democracy and Socialism

Social democracy, if realized, will betray socialism. Leaving the mechanisms of bourgeois democracy intact, it cannot unmoor itself from the structures of state capitalism. This will occur whether or not the question of the general crisis of capitalism is raised: faced with even the mildest of wealth redistribution, those that hold wealth as well as the upper strata of the middle class will oppose these policies. The lower rungs of the middle class will be enticed to support this push, formally establishing cross-class alliances that are essentially anti-socialist in nature. As we saw in Chile under Salvador Allende and the conflicts that erupted under the Sandinista government in Nicaragua, the closer to "socialism" a social-democratic government gets, the more the interests of the middle class and the upper class combine. They will carry out acts of repression aimed at maintaining the status quo, either through outright violence (in accordance with the fascist impulse) or through economic sabotage. The profit margins gained from macroeconomic stability will be momentarily impinged upon in the name of holding power. This was the nature of the alliance of the middle class and the aristocracy in Allende's Chile, who were all too willing to generate severe economic instability to undermine the popular support of the government.

Even if fascism is avoided, the combination of intentional economic unrest with the natural tendency towards economic confusion that results from greater government interference in the market means that the space between social democracy and socialism will be marked with economic crisis, resembling the general and reoccurring crises of capitalism while remaining unique and distinct. The conditions of crisis will set the oppressed classes and peoples on a march towards higher rates of exploitation and denigration; at this stage, it would appear that the maintenance of the social-democratic status quo is *in the best interests of the oppressed*, longing to be free of oppression as it stands. We find ourselves now at the increasing divergence between social self-protection and the class struggle, as self-protection comes to define itself in increasingly short-term goals. Social self-protection, in other words, begins as an expression of the class struggle but will find itself tending towards regressive strategies, even if it remains progressive in its outlook. This is the reason that Lenin, for better or worse, observed that "the working class, exclusively by its own effort, is able to develop only trade union consciousness, i.e., the conviction that it is necessary to combine in unions, fight the employers, and strive to compel the government to pass necessary labour legislation, etc."[38] From this perspective, the reality of the vanguard party seems like an inescapable conclusion.

At the same time, we must contest Lenin's essentialist claims that the worker cannot develop a "consciousness" beyond his or herself, or that they can be steered in the proper direction by "educated representatives of the propertied classes, by intellectuals." If the intellectuals of the "propertied classes" are able to develop a consciousness beyond their specific class consciousness (which, after all, is geared towards the expansion of capital accumulation), there seems little basis for the idea that a worker cannot develop a consciousness beyond short-term goals. No, the distinction lies in the actual limitations of moving past social democracy in that the capitalist system actively prohibits this passage through the intensification of its own wanton violence. In a pragmatic sense, the worker must fall back on compromise if he or she is to maintain any semblance of a standard of living. This is not through the fault of "consciousness," but the very root of the problem itself: capitalism can offer the worker happiness and welfare, which it juxtaposes against the very conditions of misery that it creates. The working class is within and against itself as much as it is within and against capitalism. "The front line no longer cuts through the middle of society; it now runs through the middle of each of us."[39] So the question remains: what is to be done? This question is by far beyond the capabilities of this short book, or any small group or person to determine, but allow us several thoughts on the matter.

How are we to define socialism? To this point, we've approached it through political economy, but allow us now to quote Henri Lefebvre:

> It is ludicrous to define socialism solely by the development of the productive forces. Economic statistics cannot answer: 'What is socialism?' Men do not fight and die for tons of steel, or for tanks or atomic bombs. They aspire to be happy, not to produce... The productive forces do not define socialism. For socialism, it is necessary for the productive forces to be at a high level, as the example of the USSR shows, but that is not enough to institute it, as the example of the USA shows... socialism (the new society, the new life) can only be concretely defined on the level of everyday life, as a system of changes in what can be called lived experience.[40]

Socialism is not simply a world in which the exploitation of the worker is ended; it is the radical negation of everything that is. In other words, the term "class struggle" itself is ultimately self-limiting, for the struggle for socialism cannot be anything but the total sum aggregate of the intersections of any and all forms of struggle against exploitation. Socialism, then, is the victory of this aggregate of struggles over any and all forms of exploitation. It speaks to the transformation of life in every way possible, to realize a higher stage of life in terms of a historical development beyond its current state. Any short-term gain – such as the capitulation to the betrayal of socialist democracy – is a bastardization of the struggle. When the inability to break fully from oppression and exploitation in capitalism becomes fully realized, the inability of any solution other than socialism organically follows, even if it is not organically acknowledged.

With this construction of the struggle for socialism – as the grand gambit of all oppressed peoples – we approach Michael Hardt and Antonio Negri's "multitude," the people who are *one but many*, that is, the assemblage "composed of innumerable internal differences that can never be reduced to a unity or an identity – different cultures, races, ethnicities, genders and sexual orientations; different forms of labor; different waves of living; different reviews of the world; and different desires. The multitude is a multiplicity of all these singular differences."[41] The multitude, in other words, embodies the spirit of socialism in that it is the proliferation of difference at its most unrestrained, capable of leading not only to slackening off of oppression but the creation of new, unexpected and unforeseeable differences. There are problems, however, with the multitude as Hardt and Negri construct it, as they find themselves in a more and more difficult position of differentiating the "communism of the multitude" from transnational neoliberalism, particularly in its more progressive veneers. This leads the two to additional problems. The first of these is a spirit of optimism, which sees the "communism of the multitude" emerging quite spontaneously from the flows of the global network society, as if it remains just barely out of reach in current society and needs only the smallest of nudges before it explodes into actualization. The multitude, like socialism, must embody the negation of the existing order; otherwise, all justifications of it cease to be.

The second problem follows from the preceding one. Unable to define themselves against capitalism in its current mode of production (a global network they dub "Empire," to differentiate it, perhaps prematurely, from the imperialism of yesteryear), they find themselves advocating the construction of a postmodern social democracy, one constructed on a global level. Hardt and Negri do note the need for approaching reform and revolution in ways separate from that of the past, writing that: "Today the historical processes of transformation are so radical that even reformist proposals can lead to revolutionary change. And when democratic reforms of the global system prove to be incapable of providing the bases of a real democracy, they demonstrate ever forcefully that a revolutionary change is needed and make it ever more possible."[42] Yet despite these words, the two offer a vision that falls strikingly short: it becomes an ode to globalized social democracy alone, one that appears simply to be World Federalism updated for the "new economy" of the information age. This is unsurprising, given that Hardt and Negri, while working in a Marxist analytic tradition, have little to say about the appropriation of surplus value on a global level, nor the spatial restructuring of the world of itself. In doing so they lose sight of the intersectionality that would give their multitude concrete form, and by extension, lose sight of any revolutionary consciousness beyond social-democratic consciousness.

The only way to sustain a revolutionary momentum through the betrayal by social democracy is to construct as many possible platforms of socialism *within* the current paradigm, prior even to any bid for social democracy. We must build "the structure of the new world in the shell of the old," as the Wobblies said.[43] In a time in which the contradiction between the natural ecosystems and the processes of production intensify with catastrophic implications, it becomes necessary to stoke the constructive imagination and begin a preemptive rebuilding of civilization through the creation of *alternative economies*, all the while warding off dangerous slippages towards the idealized "distributed capitalism" that anarcho-capitalists of a technological inclination oft proclaim. Likewise, in a time in which precarity and social marginalization promise to tighten their grip (particularly on the void of introduction of social-democratic reforms), the need to design infrastructures for mutual aid, support, solidarity, and sociality becomes more pressing than ever. And finally, in a time in which everyday life enters into an unprecedented era of degradation, distraction, boredom, anxiety, and fear, the introduction of the specter of a life beyond this life is paramount.

This is where socialism emerges: in the moment that the oppressed and exploited share a recognition of their existential condition, and take steps to strike back against it. Thus socialism realizes itself whether or not the word "socialism" is used, whether or not a word of "socialist theory" is uttered, and whether or not an exogenous factor seeks to embolden the oppressed and exploited. *Socialism is alive in both the movement and the outcome*, and yet it is not a historical inevitability. It must actively be worked for, which is why to believe in the spontaneous emergence of socialism, in any organized sense, is to fall victim to mystical idealism. No, the organization is part and parcel of the movement against capital, as the instrument that organically arises in order to strike back. This is neither the realization of a vanguard party nor the path of immediatism; it is creation and recreation of opportunity structures within and against capitalism. It is not a dialectic of "folk politics" and the politics of specialization,[44] but the conscious construction of mechanisms for *feedback* between the two aimed at shifting the cumbersome gears of hegemony. To quote Ernesto Che Guevara, the "revolution is not an apple that falls when it is ripe. You have to make it fall." We need not have to see in these words the mistakes of the past – we should see instead the unfolding of the future.

There is no guarantee that any of this comes to the end that we desire. But faced with the reality of the present the two stark choices emerge before us once again: socialism or barbarism. Both are implicit in the dynamic movements that frame our moment in history. While both can be differed and postponed, both are capable of being brought to realization through the actions of people. Given the choice, one cannot refuse, in clear conscience, to partake in the movement to cut barbarism out at its roots. All that is left, when the words of theory pale in comparison to the reality that they seek to describe, is this movement.

Notes

Chapter 1

1. Karl Marx and Frederick Engels, "The Communist Manifesto," in *The Essential Left: Marx, Engels, Lenin – Their Essential Teachings*, Barnes & Noble, 1961, pgs. 17, 19
2. On the influence of thermodynamic principles on Marx, see Amy Wendling, *Karl Marx on Technology and Alienation*, Palgrave MacMillan, 2009, pgs. 61–92
3. See Karl Polanyi, *The Great Transformation: The Political and Economic Origins of Our Time*, Beacon Press, 2001, pgs. 36–43
4. Benjamin Tucker and Clarence Lee Swartz (eds.), *Individual Liberty: Selections from the Writings of Benjamin R. Tucker*, Vanguard Press, 1926, pg. 4
5. The following explanation is adapted from the one provided in Richard D. Wolff and Stephen A. Resnick, *Contending Economic Theories: Neoclassical, Keynesian, and Marxian*, MIT Press, 2012, pgs. 171-196
6. Andrew Kliman, *Reclaiming Marx's 'Capital': A Refutation of the Myth of Inconsistency*, Lexington Books, 2006, pg. 24
7. The difference between Baran and Sweezy's "surplus" and the Marxian "surplus value" is clarified in Paul Baran and Paul Sweezy, "Last Letters: Correspondence on Some 'Theoretical Implications'," *Monthly Review*, Vol. 64, Issue 3, July–August 2012, http://monthlyreview.org/2012/07/01/last-letters/
8. Paul Baran and Paul Sweezy, *Monopoly Capitalism: An Essay on the American Economic Order and Social Order*, Monthly Review Press, 1966, pg. 108
9. Michael Roberts "Measuring the Rate of Profit, Profit Cycles, and the Next Recession," *The Next Recession*, November 2011, https://thenextrecession.files.wordpress.com/2011/11/the-profit-cycle-and-economic-recession.pdf

10. See Michael Roberts, "The cycle of profitability and the next recession," *The Next Recession*, December 18th 2012 https://thenextrecession.wordpress.com/2010/12/18/the-cycle-of-profitability-and-the-next-recession/; and George Economakis, Alexis Anastasiadis, and Maria Markaki, "An empirical investigation on the US economic performance from 1929 to 2008," International Initiative for Promoting Political Economy Annual Conference, 2010, http://www.iippe.org/wiki/images/0/01/CONF_VALUE_Anastasiadis.pdf

11. This is covered at length in Andrew Kliman, *The Failure of Capitalist Production: Underlying Causes of the Great Recession*, Pluto Press, 2011

12. Shimshon Bichler and Jonathan Nitzan, "Contours of Crisis: Plus ça change, plus c'est pareil?," *Global Research*, January 1st 2009, http://www.globalresearch.ca/contours-of-crisis/11565

13. Minqi Li, Feng Xiao, and Andong Zhu, "Long Waves, Institutional Changes, and Historical Trends: A Study of the Long-Term Movement of the Profit Rate in the Capitalist World-Economy," *Journal of World System's Research*, Vol. 13, Issue 1, 2007, http://jwsr.pitt.edu/ojs/index.php/jwsr/article/view/360

14. See Karl Marx, *Capital: A Critique of Political Economy*, Vol. 1, pgs. 104–110, https://www.marxists.org/archive/marx/works/download/pdf/Capital-Volume-I.pdf

15. Frederick Engels, "Production," *Anti-Duhring*, 1877, https://www.marxists.org/archive/marx/works/1877/anti-duhring/ch25.htm

16. Much of my discussion here has been influenced by Sam Williams, "Crisis Theories: Underconsumption," https://critiqueofcrisistheory.wordpress.com/crisis-theories-underconsumption/; and "Crisis Theories: Underconsumption (Cont'd)," https://critiqueofcrisistheory.wordpress.com/

crisis-theories-underconsumption/crisis-theories-uncon-sumption-contd/, at *Critique of Crisis Theory*

17. For a good overview of the "general glut controversy," see Fiona C. Maclachan, "The Ricardo-Malthus Debate on Underconsumption: A Case Study in Economic Conversation," *History of Political Economy*, Vol. 31, No. 3, Fall 1999, pgs. 563–574

18. Quoted in Lee H. Dymond, *A Recent History of Recognized Economic Thought: Contributions of the Nobel Laureates to Economic Science*, Lulu Publishing Services, 2015, pg. 16

19. This perspective was famously developed further in Rosa Luxemburg, *The Accumulation of Capital*, Routledge Classics, 2003

20. For an analysis of the development of Taylorism, see Hugh G. J. Aitken, *Scientific Management in Action: Taylorism at Watertown Arsenal, 1908-1915*, Princeton Legacy Library, 2014. For a Marxist critique, see Harry Braverman, *Labor and Monopoly Capital: The Degradation of Work in the Twentieth Century*, Monthly Review Press, 1998

21. Michel Aglietta, *A Theory of Capitalist Regulation: The US Experience*, Verso, 2001, pg. 358

22. Ibid

23. Joseph Schumpeter, *Business Cycles: A Theoretical, Historical, and Statistical Analysis of the Capitalist Process*, McGraw-Hill Book Company, 1939

24. Marx, *Capital*, Vol. 1, pg. 301

25. The key texts in the neo-Schumpeterian tendency are Carlota Perez, *Technological Revolutions and Finance Capital: The Dynamics of Bubbles and Golden Ages*, Edward Elgar Publishing, 2003; and Christopher Freeman and Luc Soete, *The Economics of Industrial Innovation*, Routledge, 2006

26. See Christopher Freeman and Carlota Perez, "Structural crisis of adjustment, business cycles and investment behavior," in Giovani Dosi, Christopher Freeman, Richard

Nelson, and Luc Soete (eds.), *Technical Change and Economic Theory*, Pinter Publishers, 1988, pgs. 38–66

27. Michal Kalecki, "Political Aspects of Full Employment," *Political Quarterly*, Vol. 14, Issue 4, 1943, pgs. 322–331

28. See Nicholas Crafts and Peter Fearon, "A Recession to Remember: Lessons from the US, 1937-1938," *Vox: CEPR's Policy Portal*, November 23rd 2010, http://www.voxeu.org/article/recession-remember-lessons-us-1937-1938; and Maurice W. Lee, *Economic Fluctuations*, R.D. Irwin Williams, 1995, pg. 236

29. Leon Trotsky, "The Curve of Capitalist Development," April 1923, https://www.marxists.org/archive/trotsky/1923/04/capdevel.htm

30. The classic study of pre-war planning for the postwar world is Laurance H. Shoup and William Minter, *Imperial Brain Trust: The Council on Foreign Relations and United States Foreign Policy*, Monthly Review Press, 1977

31. For an in-depth discussion, see William H. Branson, Herbert Giersch, and Peter G. Peterson, "Trends in United States International Trade and Investment since World War II," in Martin Feldstein (ed.), *The American Economy in Transition*, University of Chicago Press, 1980, pgs. 183–274

32. David Harvey, *The Condition of Postmodernity: An Enquiry Into the Origins of Cultural Change*, Wiley-Blackwell, 1991, pgs. 141–142

33. See Milton Friedman, "A Proposal for Resolving the U.S. Balance of Payments Problem: Confidential Memorandum to President-elect Richard Nixon," in Milton Friedman and Leo Melamed (eds.), *The Merits of Flexible Exchange Rates: An Anthology*, George Mason University Press, 1988, pgs. 429–438

34. Josh Biven, "Understanding the Historical Divergence Between Productivity and a Typical Worker's Pay," *Economic Policy Institute*, September 2nd 2015, http://www.epi.

org/publication/understanding-the-historic-divergence-between-productivity-and-a-typical-workers-pay-why-it-matters-and-why-its-real/

35. John Smith, "Imperialism in the Twenty-First Century," *Monthly Review*, Vol. 67, Issue 3, 2015, http://monthlyreview.org/2015/07/01/imperialism-in-the-twenty-first-century/

36. Ernest Mandel, *Long Waves of Capitalist Development: A Marxist Interpretation*, Verso, 1995

37. On immaterial labor, see Michael Hardt and Antonio Negri, *Empire*, Harvard University Press, 2000, pgs. 29–30. For two very different – yet devastating – counterpoints see Keller Easterling, *Extrastatecraft: The Power of Infrastructure Space*, Verso, 2014; and Jussi Parikka, *A Geology of Media*, University of Minnesota Press, 2015

38. "The Financial Crisis Inquiry Report: Final Report of the National Commission on the Causes of the Financial and Economic Crisis in the United States," Financial Crisis Inquiry Commission, 2011, pg. xx, http://www.gpo.gov/fdsys/pkg/GPO-FCIC/content-detail.html

39. Olivier Coibon, Yuriy Gorodnichenko, and Dmitri Koustas, "Amerisclerosis? The Puzzle of Rising U.S. Unemployment Persistence," National Bureau of Economic Research Working Paper, October 2013, http://www.brookings.edu/~/media/Projects/BPEA/Fall-2013/2013b_coibion_unemployment_persistence.pdf?la=en

40. Maria A. Arias and Yi Wen, "Recovery from the Great Recession Has Varied Around the World," Federal Reserve Bank of St. Louis, October 2015, https://www.stlouisfed.org/publications/regional-economist/october-2015/recovery-from-the-great-recession-has-varied-around-the-world

41. "Subdued Demand, Diminished Prospects," *International Monetary Fund World Economic Outlook*, January 19th 2016,

https://www.imf.org/external/pubs/ft/weo/2016/update/01/
pdf/0116.pdf

42. "Uneasy calm gives way to turbulence," *Bank for International Settlements Quarterly Review*, March 6th 2016, https://www.bis.org/publ/qtrpdf/r_qt1603a.htm

43. Eswar Prasad and Karim Foda, "October 2015 update to TIGER: Tracking indexes for the global recovery," Brookings Institution, October 2015, http://www.brookings.edu/rese arch/reports/2015/10/04-global-economic-recovery-prasad

44. "A World Awash in Money: Capital Trends through 2020," Bain & Company Inc, 2012, http://www.bain.com /images/bain_report_a_world_awash_in_money.pdf

45. Daniel Altman, "Do We Have Too Much Capital?," *Foreign Policy*, May 7th 2014, http://foreignpolicy.com/2014/05/07/do-we-have-too-much-capital/

46. Jerry Davis, "Capital Markets and Job Creation in the 21st Century," Brookings Institution, December 2015, http://www.brookings.edu/~/media/research/files/papers/20 15/12/30-21st-century-job-creation-davis/capital_ markets .pdf

47. Ibid, pg. 8

48. Ibid, pgs. 10–11

49. Ethan Pollack, "Counting Up to Green: Assessing the green economy and its implications for growth and equity," *Economic Policy Institute*, October 10th 2012, http://www. epi.org/publication/bp349-assessing-the-green-economy/

50. Anne Fisher, "Green jobs are growing, but politics get in the way," *Fortune*, March 17th 2015, http://fortune.com/2015 /03/17/green-jobs-2/

51. Kevin Carson, *The Homebrew Industrial Revolution: A Low Overhead Manifesto*, Book Surge Publishing, 2010, pgs. 89–90

52. Ben Bernanke, "Why are interest rates so low, part 3: The Global Savings Glut," *Brookings Institute Blog*, April 1st 2015, http://www.brookings.edu/blogs/ben-bernanke/posts/

2015/04/01-why-interest-rates-low-global-savings-glut

53. Michael Roberts, "Too much profit, not too little," *The Next Recession*, November 8th 2015, https://thenextrecession.word press.com/2015/11/08/too-much-profit-not-too-little/

Chapter 2

1. Johanna Brockman, *Markets in the Name of Socialism: The Left-Wing Origins of Neoliberalism*, Stanford University Press, 2013, pg. 4

2. This is covered at length in Michel Foucault, *The Birth of Biopolitics: Lectures at the College de France, 1978-1979*, Picador, 2008, see specifically pgs. 129–179

3. See Antonio Gramsci, *Selections from the Prison Notebooks*, International Publishers Company, 1971. For work that builds on Gramsci's formulations (particularly in the context of neoliberalism) see Stephen Gill, *Gramsci, Historical Materialism and International Relations*, Cambridge University Press, 1993; and William I. Robinson, *Promoting Polyarchy: Globalization, US Intervention, and Hegemony*, Cambridge University Press, 1993

4. Excellent introductions to this sociological "elite theory" are C. Wright Mills, *The Power Elite*, Oxford University Press, 2000 (reprint edition); and G. William Domhoff, *The Power Elite and the State: How Policy is Made in America*, Aldine Press, 1990

5. John Bellamy Foster and Hannah Holleman, "The Financial Power Elite," *Monthly Review*, Vol. 62, Issue 1, May 2010, http://monthlyreview.org/2010/05/01/the-financial-power-elite/

6. Giovanni Arrighi, *The Long Twentieth Century: Money, Power, and the Origins of Our Times*, Verso, 2010

7. Sara Diamond, "Right Wing Movements in the United States, 1945-1992," PhD dissertation, University of

California at Berkeley, 1993, pg. 263

8.   Ibid

9.   This is the argument advanced by Karl Polanyi, *The Great Transformation: The Political and Economic Origins of Our Time*, Beacon Press, 2001

10. Jamie Peck, *Constructions of Neoliberal Reason*, Oxford University Press, 2013, pg. 45

11. Foucault, *Birth of Biopolitics*, pg. 133

12. Quoted in Nick Srnicek and Alex Williams, *Inventing the Future: Post-Capitalism and a World Without Work*, Verso, 2015, pg. 55

13. Rob Van Horn and Philip Mirowksi, "The Rise of Chicago School Economics and the Birth of Neoliberalism," in Philip Mirowski and Dieter Plehwe (eds.), *The Road from Mont Pelerin: The Making of the Neoliberal Thought Collective*, Harvard University Press, 2009, pg. 161

14. Daniel Stedman Jones, *Masters of the Universe: Hayek, Friedman, and the Birth of Neoliberal Politics*, Princeton University Press, 2014, pg. 207

15. Each of these is covered at length in Mirowski and Plehwe (eds.), *The Road from Mont Pelerin*

16. Sara Diamond's "Right Wing Movements in the United States, 1945-1992" is an excellent primer for this history. See also Jane Mayer, *Dark Money: The Hidden History of the Billionaires Behind the Rise of the Radical Right*, Doubleday, 2016

17. Jones, *Masters of the Universe*, pg. 163

18. Ibid

19. Peck, *Constructions of Neoliberal Reason*, pg. 111

20. On the purging of Keynesians and the rise of structural-adjustment programs, see David Harvey, *A Brief History of Neoliberalism*, Oxford University Press, 2007, pgs. 22–23. For an in-depth discussion and critique of structural adjustment, see M. Rodwan Abourharb and David Cingranelli, *Human*

Rights and Structural Adjustment, Cambridge University Press, 2007

21. Nicolas Guilhot, *The Democracy Makers: Human Rights and the Politics of Global Order*, Columbia University Press, 2012, pg. 202

22. Viktor J. Vanberg, "The Freiburg School: Walter Eucken and Ordoliberalism," *Freiburg discussion papers on constitutional economics*, No. 4, 2004, pg. 4

23. Quoted in Matteo Albanese, *The Concept of War in Neoconservative Thinking*, IPOC di Pietro Condemi, 2012, pg. 56

24. Joan Roelofs, *Foundations and Public Policy: The Mask of Pluralism*, State University of New York Press, 2003, pg. 78

25. Michael G. Wilson, "The North American Free Trade Agreement: Ronald Reagan's Vision Realized," Heritage Foundation Executive Memorandum #371, 1993, http://www.heritage.org/research/reports/1993/11/em371-the-north-american-free-trade-agreement

26. Robert E. Scott, Carlos Salas, Bruce Campbell, and Jeff Faux, "Revisiting NAFTA: Still Not Working for America's Workers," Economic Policy Institute Briefing Paper, September 2006, http://www.epi.org/files/page/-/old/briefingpapers/173/bp173.pdf

27. Mark Weisbrot, Stephan Lefebvre, and Joseph Sammut, "Did NAFTA Help Mexico?," Center for Economic and Policy Research, 2014, http://cepr.net/documents/nafta-20-years-2014-02.pdf

28. Peter Edelman, "The Worst Thing Bill Clinton Has Done," *The Atlantic*, March 1997, http://www.theatlantic.com/magazine/archive/1997/03/the-worst-thing-bill-clinton-has-done/376797/

29. Case in point was Reagan's racially-coded descriptions of "welfare queens"

30. Joshua Cooper Ramo, "The Three Marketeers," *Time*,

February 15th 1999, http://content.time.com/time/world/article/0,8599,2054093,00.html

31. Quoted in Naomi Klein, *The Shock Doctrine: The Rise of Disaster Capitalism*, Picador, 2007, pg. 338

32. Anita Raghavan "Wall Street is Scavenging in Asia-Pacific" *Wall Street Journal* February 10, 1998, quoted in Ibid, pgs. 346-347

33. Giovanni Arrighi, *Adam Smith in Beijing: Lineages of the 21st Century*, Verso, 2009, pg. 195

34. See Klein, *The Shock Doctrine*, pgs. 513–534

35. Quoted in *Adam Smith in Beijing*, pg. 190

36. Donald Kagan, Gary Schmitt, and Thomas Donnelly, "Rebuilding America's Defenses: Strategy, Forces and Resources for a New Century," Project for a New American Century, September 2000, pgs. 2, 4

37. Nafeez Ahmed, "Iraqi Invasion About Oil," *The Guardian*, March 20th 2014, http://www.theguardian.com/environment/earth-insight/2014/mar/20/iraq-war-oil-resources-energy-peak-scarcity-economy

38. David Harvey, *The New Imperialism*, Oxford University Press, 2005, pg. 19

39. Quote in Klein, *The Shock Doctrine*, pg. 436

40. See Brian Holmes, "FUTURE MAP: Or, How the Cyborgs Learned How to Stop Worrying and Love Surveillance," *Continental Drift*, September 2007, https://brianholmes.wordpress.com/2007/09/09/future-map/

41. "Why Labor Wants President Bush Ousted," *Northwest Labor Press*, October 15th 2004, https://nwlaborpress.org/2004/10-15-04Bush.html

42. Peck, *Constructions of Neoliberal Rationality*, pg. 232

43. Barack Obama, *The Audacity of Hope: Thoughts on Reclaiming the American Dream*, Crown Publishers, 2006

44. Peck, *Constructions of Neoliberal Rationality*, pg. 236

45. Robert E. Scott, "No Jobs from Trade Pacts," Economic

Policy Institute, July 18th 2013, http://www.epi.org/publication/trade-pacts-korus-trans-pacific-partnership/

46. Quoted in Peck, *Constructions of Neoliberal Rationality*, pg. 251

47. Ibid, pg. 260

48. Ibid, pg. 246

49. For the effects of QE on income inequality in the UK, see Phillip Inman and Hillary Osborne, "Bank of England's recovery policies have increased inequality, finds S&P," *The Guardian*, February 10th 2016, http://www.theguardian.com/business/2016/feb/10/bank-of-englands-recovery-policies-inequality-standard-and-poors. For the effects of QE on income inequality in the US, see Jon Hartley, "How the Federal Reserve Quantitative Easing Expanded Wealth Inequality," *Forbes*, June 25th 2015, http://www.forbes.com/sites/jonhartley/2015/06/25/how-federal-reserve-quantitative-easing-expanded-wealth-inequality/

50. James K. Glassman, "Market-Based Man," *Philanthropy*, Fall 2011, http://www.philanthropyroundtable.org/topic/excellence_in_philanthropy/market_based_man

51. Ruth Milkman, Stephanie Luce, and Penny Lewis, *Changing the Subject: A Bottom-Up Account of Occupy Wall Street in New York City*, City University of New York, 2013, pg. 2, http://www.russellsage.org/research/reports/occupy-wall-street-movement

52. The dynamics of the relationship between organized labor and Occupy are probed in depth in Suzanne Collado, "Occupy's Alliance with Labor," *Is This What Democracy Looks Like?*, http://what-democracy-looks-like.com/occupys-alliance-with-labor-2/

53. Milkman, Luce, and Lewis, *Changing the Subject*, pg. 20

54. Ibid, pg. 18

55. Michael Gould-Wartofsky, "From the People's House to Zuccotti Park," *Jacobin*, February 2015, https://www.jac

obinmag.com/2015/02/occupy-wall-street-wisconsin/

56. See Hamid Dabashi, *The Arab Spring: The End of Postcolonialism*, Zed Books, 2012

57. For good insight into the alter-globalization movement, see Eddie Yuen, Daniel-Burton Rose, and George Katsiaficas, *Confronting Capitalism: Dispatches from a Global Movement*, Soft Skull Press, 2004

58. All data from *Open Secrets*, https://www.opensecrets.org/

59. Debbie Dooley, "Tea Party Founder: Why I Support Donald Trump for President," January 25th 2016, http://www. breitbart.com/big-government/2016/01/25/why-i-support-donald-trump-for-president/

60. Doug Mataconis, "Tea Party Apparently Now Considers Stopping Immigration Reform Most Important Issue," *Outside the Beltway*, July 15th 2013, http://www.outsidethe-beltway.com/tea-party-apparently-now-considers-stopping-immigration-reform-most-important-issue/

61. Ben Schreckinger, "White supremacist groups see Trump bump," *Politico*, December 2015, http://www.politico .com/story/2015/12/donald-trump-white-supremacists-216620

62. Matthew Vadum, "Occupy Wall Street Returns to Help Bernie," *Frontpage Mag*, April 18th 2016, http://www.front-pagemag.com/fpm/262543/occupy-wall-street-returns-help-bernie-matthew-vadum

63. Arit John, "For 'Occupy' alums, Sanders is just a means to an end," *Chicago Tribune*, April 15th 2016, http://www.chicagot ribune.com/news/sns-wp-blm-sanders-supporters-fc52b8 14-031c-11e6-8bb1-f124a43f84dc-20160415-story.html

64. Lily Geismer, "Atari Democrats," *Jacobin*, February 2016, https://www.jacobinmag.com/2016/02/geismer-democratic-party-atari-tech-silicon-valley-mondale/

65. Ibid

66. See William A. Galston, "Trump Rides a Blue-Collar Wave,"

The Wall Street Journal, November 17th 2015, http://www.wsj.com/articles/trump-rides-a-blue-collar-wave-14478 03248

Chapter 3

1.   Karl Polanyi, *The Great Transformation: The Political and Economic Origins of Our Times,* Beacon Press, 2001, pg. 136
2.   See Matthew C. MacWilliams, "Donald Trump is attracting authoritarian primary voters, and it may help him to gain the nomination," *London School of Economics US Centre,* January 27th 2016, http://blogs.lse.ac.uk/usappblog/20 16/01/27/donald-trump-is-attracting-authoritarian-primary-voters-and-it-may-help-him-to-gain-the-nomination/
3.   Chip Bertlet and Matthew Lyons, *Right-Wing Populism in America: Too Close for Comfort,* The Guilford Press, 2000, pg. 286
4.   "Quotation of the Day," *The New York Times,* February 14th 2000, http://www.nytimes.com/2000/02/14/nyregion/quotati on-of-the-day-815233.html
5.   Chris Cillizza, "Pat Buchanan says Donald Trump is the future of the Republican Party," *The Washington Post,* January 12th 2016, https://www.washingtonpost.com /news/the-fix/wp/2016/01/12/pat-buchanan-believes-donald-trump-is-the-future-of-the-republican-party/
6.   Patrick Buchanan, "How Free Trade is Killing the Middle Class," *The American Conservative,* January 24th 2015, http://www.theamericanconservative.com/2014/01/24/free-trade-middle-america/
7.   Llewelyn Rockwell, Jr, "The Case for Paleo-Libertarianism," *Liberty,* Vol. 3, No. 3, January 1990, pg. 37, http://www.liber-tyunbound.com/sites/files/printarchive/Liberty_Magazine_J anuary_1990.pdf
8.   Murray Rothbard, "Right-Wing Populism: A Strategy for the

Paleo Movement," *Rothbard-Rockwell Report*, Vol. 3, No. 1, January 1992, pg. 5, http://rothbard.altervista.org/artic les/right-wing-populism.pdf

9. Quoted in Lee Edwards, *The Conservative Revolution: The Movement that Remade America*, The Free Press, 1999, pg. 329

10. Rajani Palme Dutt, *Fascism and Social Revolution: A Study of the Economics and Politics of the Extreme Stages of Capitalism in Decay*, International Publishers, 1935, pg. 208

11. This is covered in Fred Turner, *The Democratic Surround: Multimedia and American Liberalism from World War II to the Psychedelic Sixties*, University of Chicago Press, 2013

12. Tending in this direction would be Yann Moulier-Boutang, *Cognitive Capitalism*, Polity, 2012

13. Quoted in Dutt, *Fascism and Social Revolution*, pgs. 180–181

14. Michal Kalecki, "Political Aspects of Full Employment," *MRZine*, September 22nd 2010 (reprint), http://mrzine.mo nthlyreview.org/2010/kalecki220510.html

15. Sebastian Budgen and Costas Lapavitsas, "Greece: Phase 2," https://www.jacobinmag.com/2015/03/lapavitsas-varoufakis-grexit-syriza/

16. Michal Kalecki, *Selected Essays on Economic Planning*, Cambridge University Press, 2011, pg. 20

17. Bernie Sanders, "An Economic Agenda for America: 12 Steps Forward," *Huffington Post*, January 31st 2015, http://www. huffingtonpost.com/rep-bernie-sanders/an-economic-agenda-for-am_b_6249022.html

18. "Labor Leadership Statements," The Co-operative Party, September 14th 2015, https://party.coop/2015/09/14/8679/

19. See, for example, Gar Alperovitz and Keane Bhatt, "What Then Can I Do? Ten Ways to Democratize the Economy," *Truthout*, September 24th 2013, http://www.truth-out.org/ opinion/item/18908-what-then-can-i-do-ten-steps-toward-transforming-the-system

20. See Michel Bauwens, "Blueprint for P2P Society: The Partner

State & Ethical Economy," *Shareable,* April 7th 2012, http://www.shareable.net/blog/blueprint-for-p2p-society-the-partner-state-ethical-economy

21. Giles Tremlett, "Basque co-op protects itself with buffer of foreign workers," *The Guardian,* October 23rd 2007, http://www.theguardian.com/business/2001/oct/23/global-recession.internationalnews

22. For an excellent overview of the Yugoslavian approach to Marxist theory, see Fred Warner Neal, *Titoism in Action: The Reforms in Yugoslavia After 1948,* University of California Press, 1958, pgs. 15–33

23. Johanna Brockman, *Markets in the Name of Socialism: The Left-Wing Origins of Neoliberalism,* Stanford University Press, 2013, pg. 102

24. This is discussed at length in Joseph Stiglitz, *Whither Socialism?,* MIT Press, 1996

25. Rosa Luxemburg, *Reform or Revolution and Other Writings,* Dover Publications, 2006, pgs. 22–23

26. "The Gotha Program," 1875, *German History in Documents and Images, Volume 4. Forging an Empire: Bismarckian Germany, 1866-1890,* https://www.archive.org/stream/GothaProgramme/726_socWrkrsParty_gothaProgram_231_djvu.txt

27. Karl Marx and Frederick Engels, "Critique of the Gotha Program," 1875, in Karl Marx and Frederick Engels, *Marx/Engels Selected Works,* Vol. 3, Progress Publishers, 1970, pgs. 13–30, https://www.marxists.org/archive/marx/works/1875/gotha/

28. Ibid

29. Erfurt Program, 1891, https://www.marxists.org/history/international/social-democracy/1891/erfurt-program.htm

30. Rudolph Hilferding, *Finance Capital: A Study of the Latest Phase of Capitalist Development,* 1910, http://www.marxists.org/archive/hilferding/1910/finkap/ch25.htm

31. Joseph Schumpeter, *Capitalism, Socialism, Democracy,* Harper

Perennial Modern Classics, 2008 (reprint edition), pg. 162

32. Ludwig von Mises, *Liberalism: A Socio-Economic Exposition*, Sheed, Andrews, and McMeel (eds.), 1978, pg. 51

33. See, for example, Ron Paul, "Democracy =/= Freedom," *Ron Paul Revolution*, August 27th 2012, http://www.ronpaul .com/2012-08-27/ron-paul-democracy-%E2%89%A0-freedom/

34. See Helmut Gruber, *Red Vienna: Experiments in Working-Class Culture*, Oxford University Press, 1991

35. Vladimir Lenin and Todd Chretien (trans.), *The State and Revolution*, Haymarket Books, 2014, pg. 43

36. Nick Srnicek and Alex Williams, *Inventing the Future: Postcapitalism and a Work Without Work*, Verso, 2015, pg. 108

37. Marx and Engels, "Critique of the Gotha Program"

38. Vladimir Lenin, "What is to be Done? Burning Questions for Our Movement," 1902, in Vladimir Lenin (author), Joe Finberg, and George Hanna (trans.), *Lenin's Collected Works*, Foreign Languages Publishing House, 1961, pgs. 347–530, https://www.marxists.org/archive/lenin/works/1901/witbd/

39. Tiqqun, *This Is Not a Program*, Semiotext(e), 2011, pg. 12

40. Henri Lefebvre, *The Critique of Everyday Life*, Vol. 1, Verso, 1991, pgs. 48–49

41. Michael Hardt and Antonio Negri, *Multitude: War and Democracy in the Age of Empire*, Penguin Press, 2004, pg. xiv

42. Ibid, pg. 289

43. "Preamble to the IWW Constitution," http://www.iww .org/culture/official/preamble.shtml

44. Different dimensions of this dialectic can be analyzed in a multitude of ways. For the disruptive effects of "top-down" knowledge, see James C. Scott, *Seeing Like a State: How Certain Schemes to Improve the Human Condition Have Failed*, Yale University Press, 1999. For the importance of specialized knowledge and expertise, see Srnicek and Williams, *Inventing the Future*. For a work that builds to a

resolution to this conflict, see McKenzie Wark, *Molecular Red: Theory for the Anthropocene*, Verso, 2015. My own considerations on this dialectic will be the subject of a forthcoming book; in the meantime, see my "Learning the Future: Bogdanov, Neurath, and Scientific Socialism," *Deterritorial Investigations Unit*, December 29th 2015, https://deterritorial-investigations.wordpress.com/2015/12/29/learning-the-future-bogdanov-neurath-and-scientific-socialism/

Zero Books

CULTURE, SOCIETY & POLITICS

Contemporary culture has eliminated the concept and public figure of the intellectual. A cretinous anti-intellectualism presides, cheer-led by hacks in the pay of multinational corporations who reassure their bored readers that there is no need to rouse themselves from their stupor. Zer0 Books knows that another kind of discourse - intellectual without being academic, popular without being populist - is not only possible: it is already flourishing. Zer0 is convinced that in the unthinking, blandly consensual culture in which we live, critical and engaged theoretical reflection is more important than ever before.

If you have enjoyed this book, why not tell other readers by posting a review on your preferred book site. Recent bestsellers from Zero Books are:

In the Dust of This Planet
Horror of Philosophy vol. 1
Eugene Thacker
In the first of a series of three books on the Horror of Philosophy, *In the Dust of This Planet* offers the genre of horror as a way of thinking about the unthinkable.
Paperback: 978-1-84694-676-9 ebook: 978-1-78099-010-1

Capitalist Realism
Is there no alternative?
Mark Fisher
An analysis of the ways in which capitalism has presented itself as the only realistic political-economic system.
Paperback: 978-1-84694-317-1 ebook: 978-1-78099-734-6

Rebel Rebel
Chris O'Leary
David Bowie: every single song. Everything you want to know, everything you didn't know.
Paperback: 978-1-78099-244-0 ebook: 978-1-78099-713-1

Cartographies of the Absolute
Alberto Toscano, Jeff Kinkle
An aesthetics of the economy for the twenty-first century.
Paperback: 978-1-78099-275-4 ebook: 978-1-78279-973-3

Malign Velocities
Accelerationism and Capitalism
Benjamin Noys
Long listed for the Bread and Roses Prize 2015, *Malign Velocities* argues against the need for speed, tracking acceleration as the symptom of the on-going crises of capitalism.
Paperback: 978-1-78279-300-7 ebook: 978-1-78279-299-4

Meat Market
Female flesh under Capitalism
Laurie Penny
A feminist dissection of women's bodies as the fleshy fulcrum of capitalist cannibalism, whereby women are both consumers and consumed.
Paperback: 978-1-84694-521-2 ebook: 978-1-84694-782-7

Poor but Sexy
Culture Clashes in Europe East and West
Agata Pyzik
How the East stayed East and the West stayed West.
Paperback: 978-1-78099-394-2 ebook: 978-1-78099-395-9

Romeo and Juliet in Palestine
Teaching Under Occupation
Tom Sperlinger
Life in the West Bank, the nature of pedagogy and the role of a
university under occupation.
Paperback: 978-1-78279-637-4 ebook: 978-1-78279-636-7

Sweetening the Pill
or How we Got Hooked on Hormonal Birth Control
Holly Grigg-Spall
Has contraception liberated or oppressed women? *Sweetening
the Pill* breaks the silence on the dark side of hormonal
contraception.
Paperback: 978-1-78099-607-3 ebook: 978-1-78099-608-0

Readers of ebooks can buy or view any of these
bestsellers by clicking on the live link in the title. Most
titles are published in paperback and as an ebook.
Paperbacks are available in traditional bookshops. Both
print and ebook formats are available online.

Find more titles and sign up to our readers' newsletter at
http://www.johnhuntpublishing.com/culture-and-politics.
Follow us on Facebook at
https://www.facebook.com/ZeroBooks
and Twitter at https://twitter.com/Zer0Books.